Pure Living
How to Detox Your Home

Pure Living

How to Detox Your Home

Sally Bevan

Sally Bevan is a freelance journalist and writer who specializes in green issues, interiors and buildings. Her work has appeared in the *Guardian*, the *Independent* and the *Evening Standard*. She is also the author of *The Reclaimers*, a book accompanying the new BBC2 series.

For more information on the author, visit her website at www.sallybevan.com

Photo © Al Bevan 2004

Medical consultant: Dr David Bull MBBS, BSc(i)

Published by BBC Worldwide Ltd, Woodlands, 80 Wood Lane, London W12 0TT

First published in 2004 for Marks & Spencer plc
This edition first published in 2005

ISBN 0 563 52170 8

Commissioning Editor: Vivien Bowler
Project Editor: Sarah Lavelle
Copy Editor: Ruth Baldwin
Art Director: Sarah Ponder
Design: Grade Design Consultants
Picture Researcher: Victoria Hall

Set in Helvetica Neue and OCRB
Printed and bound by LEGO SpA
Colour separations by Radstock Reproductions Ltd

For more information about this and other BBC books, please telephone 08700 777 001 or visit our website on www.bbc.shop.com

Contents

1

Detox

Our homes are sanctuaries, places of shelter and sanity. They shield us from the elements and make us feel safe. We make them the focus for family life, a centre for important daily activities – eating, relaxing, sleeping, raising children, washing and, for an increasing number of us, working.

Unfortunately, some of the things we use in our homes can damage our wellbeing. There are hundreds of chemicals and synthetic materials found in paints, furnishings, electrical goods, cosmetics, food and other household items. Many of these have been linked to headaches, asthma, skin irritation and other more serious medical problems. They also pose a significant threat to the environment. Added to this, poor lighting, inadequate ventilation and uncomfortable furniture make us feel out of tune with our living space.

So, if you've been putting that persistent headache down to too much red wine or resigned yourself to a life of feeling tired all the time, think again. Take a closer look at your living space because it might just be time to detox your home.

There is a natural connection between healthy homes and healthy bodies. Just as we are what we eat, so 'we are where we live'. Conditions such as sick building syndrome, stress and Seasonal Affective Disorder (SAD) are linked to how we interact with our homes. We all want comfortable, healthy and beautiful homes, but it seems many of us are struggling.

Thankfully the solution is simple. The answer doesn't involve uprooting and moving to an eco-house in the wilderness, nor will you have to empty out your home and start again. It's the little choices you make on a daily basis that will have the most positive impact on the environment, your living space and, most importantly, your wellbeing.

But this book isn't just about focusing on home health troublespots or saving the planet. It's about transforming a house into a haven. *Pure Living* will show you how to change your bathroom into an indulgent home spa or turn a boring bedroom into a slumber sanctuary. After all, you'll be sleeping soundly in the knowledge that your home is now a place of health and harmony, for you and all your family.

The unhealthy home

People spend vast amounts decorating their houses. You only have to attempt a Sunday outing to a DIY store to see this is true. We pore over lifestyle magazines, tune into home make-over television programmes in our millions and spend every last drop of disposable income turning our pads into paradises. And the results are impressive. Never before has a generation been so interested in good design and daring decoration.

Unfortunately, although many of us are paying a great deal of attention to the appearance of our homes, few are aware of the hidden costs involved in modern home living. Yes, our houses are 'safer' than they have ever been in terms of fire safety, building regulations and sanitation. But alongside these positive improvements, new synthetic materials, household chemicals and certain technologies have brought their own sets of problems.

At home, at school and in the office people have started to complain about recurrent symptoms including headaches, allergies, fatigue and breathing difficulties. Scientists investigating these problems have found, rather shockingly, that air pollution is often worse inside rather than outside a house. Studies by the UK Building Research Establishment (BRE) showed that the indoor air quality in rural Avon was ten times worse than outdoors. The BRE found more than 200 chemicals in the air within buildings, of which 80 were deemed to have adverse health effects. Similar studies have revealed that the same is true in cities worldwide. In a study that began in 1980 Lance Wallace, a scientist working for the US Environmental Protection Agency, measured exposure to environmental pollutants in more than 2000 people who lived in or around twelve American cities. His conclusions were the same. For most pollutants in the study, the air outside was safer to breathe than air inside the home.

But how is this possible? Homes are supposed to be havens, refuges from the stresses and strains of modern living. Why are they making us ill?

Every day, it seems, we absorb a cocktail of chemicals and toxins. Studies monitoring the quality of air in our homes and workplaces found a worrying mix of pollutants including formaldehyde, carbon monoxide, micro-organisms and tobacco smoke. Wood panelling, cigarettes, medium density fibreboard (MDF), insulation, plywood, carpets, fabrics, paints, cleaning products and heating fuel are some of the prime suspects.

In addition to poor air quality, chemicals found in other household items such as food, cosmetics and shampoos are adding to the toxic overload. Take childhood eczema, for example. A condition that was barely heard of in the 1950s now affects one in five children. Leading dermatologists based at Sheffield University traced the origins of this rise to many of the 'wonders' of modern life, including bubble baths, shower gels and baby wipes. Products like these contain strong perfumes and surfactants (which help liquids to foam or penetrate solids more easily), both of which can trigger eczema, according to the study.

On top of these problems we also have to deal with biological contaminants in the home. Central heating, double glazing and carpets have produced warmer, more comfortable homes, both for humans and for allergy-causing dust mites. Buildings old and new also harbour mould, animal dander (small scales from animal skin) and pollen, all of which can trigger allergic reactions and lead to health problems. Added to that the burden of other factors such as noise pollution and electromagnetic radiation and it's easy to see how a house can suffer from a condition that's become commonly known as 'sick building syndrome'.

What is...sick building syndrome?

A term first used in the 1980s to explain why office workers were developing headaches, sore eyes and respiratory problems. Scientists discovered that airtight buildings, designed to keep heat in and cold out, trapped in hazardous fumes from new carpets, paints, office equipment and other sources.

GETTING STARTED
How toxic is your home?

Do you think your house might be adversely affecting your wellbeing? Below are some common symptoms associated with toxins in the home.

Tick any symptoms that you or any member of your household suffers from on a regular basis. Pay special attention to any symptoms that started when you moved to a new house or that coincided with redecorating, recarpeting or refurbishing your existing home. Also take note of any symptoms that seem to improve when you leave your house for a few days or when you stop using a particular product, such as a shampoo or air freshener.

If symptoms persist even after you've made changes, you should seek medical advice. The more boxes you have ticked, the more important it is to get to the bottom of the problem and to establish whether anything in your house could be to blame. Use the following chapters to help you identify and minimize potential hazards in your home.

Some changes may have an immediately beneficial effect – changing your shampoo might instantly reduce any scalp irritation you've been experiencing, for example. Others may take longer to show their benefits. Some of the suggestions in this book are also preventive, such as reducing your intake of pesticide residues on food or checking for radon gas, and will help you lower the risk of certain health problems developing in the future.

You	Partner	Children	
☐	☐	☐	**Breathing problems (wheezing, coughing, shortness of breath, etc.)**
☐	☐	☐	**Drowsiness**
☐	☐	☐	**Dry or irritated throat**

You	Partner	Children	
☐	☐	☐	Fatigue
☐	☐	☐	Feeling sick
☐	☐	☐	General malaise
☐	☐	☐	Headaches
☐	☐	☐	Itchy or sore eyes
☐	☐	☐	Inability to concentrate
☐	☐	☐	Insomnia
☐	☐	☐	Irritability
☐	☐	☐	Joint pains
☐	☐	☐	Light-headedness
☐	☐	☐	Nasal irritation
☐	☐	☐	Sinus problems
☐	☐	☐	Skin rashes
☐	☐	☐	Sneezing

Are you affected?

You may have gone through the checklist on pages 10–11 with other members of your family and found that not everyone was suffering from the same symptoms. It might be the case that one of you experiences quite a few of these problems while another family member, living under the same roof, is totally unaffected. Does this automatically mean that the house or its contents can't be to blame for your symptoms?

Not necessarily. People can differ in their sensitivity to toxic chemicals and irritants. Everyone has their own personal threshold and even this can change over time. Stress, lack of sleep or a chronic infection, for instance, can alter a person's threshold to the amount of contaminants he or she can cope with. For example, some people notice that when they are under stress they become more allergic to certain substances in everyday brands of shampoo, soaps and shower gel.

People can also have a bad reaction to a substance but become so used to it that they are no longer aware of any problem. In other words, you simply stop noticing that you always have a runny nose or itchy eyes. The immune system is still working hard to fight the pollutant, but continued exposure will leave your body exhausted and depressed. Doctors in the United States, for example, have suggested that ME (myalgic encephalomyelitis) or chronic fatigue syndrome could be a result of multiple factors 'weighing down' the immune system, causing it to become unbalanced. These factors include exposure to mercury dental fillings, aluminium, pesticides, chemical pollutants, electromagnetic pollution from power lines, and food intolerances.

What should you do?

There's a good chance that you've gone through the 'How toxic is your home?' checklist and suspect that there might be a few areas of your home life adversely affecting your health. Even if you haven't been experiencing any problems, you may want to prevent any from developing in the future. The question is what to do now?

There's very little consensus among scientists, companies and the government about this issue. Over 60 top independent scientists from across Europe recently supported the international wildlife organization WWF's campaign to remove or control hazardous man-made chemicals from the home (see www.wwf.org.uk) and yet other scientists claim that there is little or no problem. This means that you have to decide how seriously you want to take the problem. Some people feel that since the professionals can't decide on the facts, you might as well ignore the problem and get on with your life as – who knows – you might get run over by the number 11 bus tomorrow.

Other people are much more concerned, to the point of advocating total avoidance of all synthetic materials and chemicals in the home. This might be necessary for very chemically sensitive people but presents a tough challenge for most of us. Life is stressful enough without having to spenc every waking moment worrying that our carpets might be killing us or feeling scared to walk through the front door.

The solution needs to be realistic. Few of us can afford to up sticks and move to an eco-house or rip out every last piece of furnishing and start again. Neither should you feel overwhelmed by guilt or panic. Little steps sometimes have just as much impact as bigger ones and any change is good. That's why there's a PURE LIVING PRIORITY box at the end of each chapter, to encourage even the busiest reader to make a positive step towards pure living.

For those of us who want to take a more comprehensive approach, I've included a mix of quick fixes and longer-term solutions from which you can pick and choose as you wish. Many of the changes you will be able to make overnight, such as swapping to organic milk or plant-based cosmetics, whereas others might have to be made over a longer period, when time and money allow. Some of the *Pure Living* recommendations are also very pleasurable and a treat in themselves – the home spa, for example (see pages 29–31), is the perfect way both to destress and detox at the same time. The key is to do what you can, as even the smallest changes will bring cumulative and far-reaching benefits for you and your family.

PURE LIVING PRIORITY

If you do only one thing...

...check the products you and your family use in the home. Could these be contributing to an unhealthy environment?

2

Wash

The bathroom is the perfect place for private indulgence. From the refreshing blast of a morning shower to a soothing candlelit soak, we have transformed the mundane necessities of washing and grooming into a pleasurable daily ritual. But how therapeutic would you find your pampering routine if you knew that your shower gel contained a detergent so powerful it's used to clean industrial equipment or that your hairspray might be interfering with your hormones? In recent years consumers have put their faith in the natural beauty market. Companies such as Aveda and Neal's Yard Remedies, using fewer synthetic chemicals and more organically grown ingredients, provide customers with what they regard as safer, more eco- and body-friendly products. But is the fuss really justified?

Are you the sensitive type?

Certainly natural beauty products are popular with those who have sensitive skin or allergies to synthetic ingredients. According to research, between 50 and 90 per cent of us consider ourselves to be 'sensitive' to certain cosmetics. Many of us say we regularly experience skin irritation, redness, itching or spots, often after trying a new product – a moisturizer, lipstick or hair dye, for example.

The chances of an adverse reaction to a new beauty product are increased by the amount of indoor pollution in your home. 'It does seem there's a connection between indoor and outdoor environmental pollution and the incidence of sensitized skin,' says Dr Diana Howard from the International Dermal Institute.

So it's a chemical double whammy. An unhealthy home is more likely to give you sensitive skin, which is in turn more likely to react badly to synthetic chemicals found in conventional bath products and cosmetics. It's little wonder that so many people are making the link between healthy homes, healthy products and healthy bodies.

More than skin deep

However, skin rashes, sensitivity and spots aren't the only problems associated with chemicals in cosmetics. Dr Jurgen Klein, co-founder of the naturopathic health and beauty company Jurlique, believes he can cite 'over 150 ingredients suspected of causing cancer that are still used in over-the-counter cosmetics'. Sounds alarming, doesn't it?

It's no secret that a large number of chemicals commonly used in toiletries have been found to cause cancer in rodents or to disrupt hormones, but the cosmetics industry insists that the amounts of such substances are minute and are well below the levels needed to cause health problems in humans. The safety of these chemicals is also tightly controlled by government legislation.

But while the odd pot of face cream isn't likely to cause you any harm, environmental and health campaigners believe that we just don't know enough about the effects of continuous daily contact with these chemicals to say that all toiletries are totally safe. Helen Lynn, from the Women's Environmental Network, points out that: 'Nobody has tested the effects of repeated, long-term exposure to a mixture of chemicals from our daily routines of cleansing, moisturizing, deodorizing and applying make-up.' They believe we should take a much more precautionary approach.

Take sodium lauryl sulphate (SLS), for example. SLS is used in almost all bathroom products including toothpaste, bubble bath, shampoo and shower gel, and its side effects have long been argued over. A recent American College of Toxicology report stated that SLS appears to be safe in formulations designed for discontinuous, brief use followed by thorough rinsing from the surface of the skin. Yet how many children, asks US natural beauty guru Linda Chaé, have a 'discontinuous, brief' bubble bath?

But this is not only a health issue. We wash many litres of chemicals down the sink plughole every day, polluting the environment and poisoning wildlife. Alkylphenol ethoxylates, used in shampoos, hair colours and shaving gels, for instance, are known to be extremely toxic to fish.

Steps in the right direction

To be fair to manufacturers of beauty products, however, much of what we are learning about chemicals in cosmetics is the result of quite recent research. As scientists discover potential problems with a variety of chemicals, companies often have to play catch-up. Recently the environmental charity Friends of the Earth (FoE) challenged UK high-street retailers about their use of chemicals and toxins. As a result, five companies – Marks & Spencer, Boots, the Co-op, B&Q and the Early Learning Centre – agreed to back the charity's 'Risky Chemicals Pledge'. By doing this, all five companies took a positive step and made a commitment to their customers to identify which products contain harmful chemicals and phase out these risky substances within five years.

Many individuals and companies are also making efforts to look for alternatives while others are waiting for definitive proof that a chemical is harmful. Parabens, for example, are preservatives widely used in the cosmetic industry. Concerns about the effect of parabens on human health are widespread, but there are few viable alternatives available at the moment, unless customers are willing to buy toiletries with a short shelf life. A company won't reformulate its products based on incomplete scientific data and it can take years of research to find a suitable alternative that customers will buy. How many of us, for example, have tried natural toothpaste and instantly liked the taste? Chemical-free beauty products, like many other organic changes, can be an acquired taste.

What's more, most shops won't sell organic or chemical-free beauty products unless the customer asks for them. It's the age-old problem of supply and demand. If your favourite beauty store doesn't stock natural products, ask them why. It sounds like a cliché, but your till receipt can be as influential as your vote when it comes to promoting pure living.

Care of your skin

You may not be aware that your skin absorbs as much as 60 per cent of what is applied to it – hence the effectiveness of nicotine patches, for example. But this sponge-like quality also means that you should be careful about what you put on your body in the name of beauty. In fact, you should choose your cosmetics, soaps and body lotions as carefully as the things you eat and drink: it's estimated that over the course of a year, the average woman may absorb up to 2 kg (4 lb) of chemicals from her toiletries.

Become a bathroom detective

Campaigners, including the Consumers' Association, also want to see plainer labelling on products so that consumers aren't bamboozled by chemical names. Take a look at the ingredients list on the back of any shampoo or hand-wash and you'd be forgiven for thinking you needed a degree in chemistry to make any sense of it. Without specialist knowledge how on earth are you expected to tell your *Arachis hypogaea* (peanut oil) from your methyl paraben, a preservative thought to trigger skin irritation in certain people?

The UK cosmetics industry is regulated by the Department of Trade and Industry, which requires that manufacturers must list all of the ingredients in a product. However, fragrance chemicals, which are used to make cosmetics smell nice, are excluded and can be listed under the general term 'parfum' (or 'fragrance' in the USA). According to the Consumers' Association, more than 2500 chemicals can be listed simply as 'parfum', despite the fact that over 20 of these have been identified by the European Union Scientific Committee in Cosmetics and Non-Food Products as a common cause of allergies.

What are...'natural' and 'organic'?

In theory 'natural' refers to products that exist in nature, but in practice the word means very little when used to describe cosmetics and toiletries. In most countries very few ingredients need to be natural for this word to be used to sell a product – sometimes as little as 1 per cent.

'Organic', on the other hand, describes a product that has been certified as grown without the use of artificial pesticides and fertilizers. In the UK look for beauty products that carry the Soil Association Organic Standard symbol or the mark of another reputable certifier (see 'Useful addresses', pages 129–37).

PURE SHOPPING Dr Hauschka

If you want truly natural beauty products, look no further than Dr Hauschka. Dubbed 'the Birkenstock of beauty' by *W* magazine, this German enterprise recently became a favourite with eco-warriors and A-list celebrities alike because of its über-natural products and respect for the environment.

FOR MORE INFORMATION, see 'Useful addresses', page 133.

Founded more than 30 years ago by Dr Hauschka, a chemist and creator of herbal remedies, the company believes strongly in the relationship between high-quality natural ingredients and healthy bodies. Almost every plant ingredient is sown and grown according to biodynamic principles, a type of organic farming that works in harmony with the rhythms of nature and the universe. Seeds are planted according to the position of the planets and flowers are picked at sunrise to capture their full 'life force'. After harvesting, a special extraction process preserves and strengthens the living essence of the processed plants and herbs, which are then turned into nourishing skin creams, delicious-smelling facial oils and refreshing hair-care products. The results speak for themselves: according to glossy-magazine gossip, the range is a huge hit both here and stateside, with celebrities including Julia Roberts, Cate Blanchett and Madonna choosing Hauschka natural beauty over synthetic products.

Getting started
Take a toxic tour of your bathroom

Until cosmetic labelling becomes easier to decipher you'll need to become a keen label reader. This isn't as laborious as it sounds – once you've looked at a few toiletries you'll begin to recognize the same ingredients in a wide variety of products.

Below you'll find a list of common chemicals used in toiletries that have been targeted by consumer groups. Some campaigners believe that toiletries and cosmetics contain so many unsafe chemicals that we are literally washing our money and our wellbeing down the drain. The jury is still out on most of these chemicals, so rather than run screaming from your bathroom, why not simply reduce your exposure to them or look for more natural alternatives?

Fragrance
Found in: Most personal-care products.
Purpose: To make cosmetics smell nice.
Words to look out for: Fragrance chemicals appear as 'parfum' in the EU or 'fragrance' in the USA.

The scents in perfumes, soaps, creams and shaving foam are formed by combining many different fragrances, sometimes up to 300 at a time. While only a few of these fragrances seem to provoke allergy, the problem is that they are present in the majority of products. Fragrance has also been linked to breathing difficulties, allergies and multiple chemical sensitivities according to the Women's Environmental Network (www.wen.org.uk). Fragrance is the cause of most allergic reactions to a cosmetic.

Artificial colours

Found in: Beauty products, especially make-up and hair dye.
Purpose: To make a product look more attractive.
Words to look out for: In UK beauty products, both natural and artificial colours are represented by the letters 'Cl' followed by a number: for example, 'Cl 61570'. In the USA look for the letters 'FD&C' or 'D&C' followed by a colour and a number: for instance, 'FD&C Red No.6'.

Nearly all of the colours found in medicine, toothpaste and cosmetics are synthetic. Some cause no reaction, others have been associated with health problems including attention deficit disorder, hyperactivity and skin irritation. For example, paraphenylenediamine is a colour regularly used in dark hair dye and can cause severe reactions on the scalp, eyelids, upper ears and face of people with sensitive skin.

Benzene

Found in: Lacquers, nail varnishes and cosmetics.
Purpose: Used as a solvent.

Benzene is a petrochemical that is highly toxic even in minute proportions and has known carcinogenic (cancer-causing) properties. Avoid if possible.

Formaldehyde

Found in: Deodorants, shampoos, hand-washes, nail varnishes and other cosmetics.
Purpose: Used as a disinfectant, germicide, fungicide, defoamer and preservative.
Words to look out for: Formaldehyde, formalin, formal and methyl aldehyde.

According to the US Environmental Protection Agency, formaldehyde can irritate the eyes, nose and throat, and may also trigger asthma in sensitive individuals. Skin reactions after exposure to formaldehyde are common because the chemical is both irritating and allergy-causing. It is classified as a potential carcinogen and has been shown to produce mutations and abnormal organisms in laboratory studies. Its use is restricted in many countries.

Phthalates

Found in: Hairspray, perfumes and nail varnishes.

Purpose: Used to make nail varnish chip-resistant. Also used in hairspray to add flexibility and added to perfume to prevent evaporation.

Words to look out for: Dibutylphthalate (DBP), dimethylphthalate (DMP) and diethylphthalate (DEP).

Phthalates (pronounced 'tha-lates') have been criticized for acting as hormone disruptors. They have been linked with premature breast development in young girls and faulty reproductive development in male foetuses. Phthalates may also be linked to asthma, liver and kidney damage. Environmental and consumer groups say the current research indicates that the use of phthalates could be a health hazard, so the safest move would be to phase out such chemicals. Cosmetic industry groups believe studies have not conclusively proven the chemicals to be dangerous. The position held by the US Food and Drug Administration on whether phthalates affect human health is: 'We don't know.'

Triclosan

Found in: Deodorants, toothpastes, vaginal washes, liquid soaps, mouth-washes.

Purpose: Anti-bacterial.

Words to look out for: Sometimes listed as '5-chloro2-(2,4-dichlorophenoxy)-phenol'.

The American Medical Association believes that triclosan is capable of causing anti-microbial resistance in the same way that indiscriminate prescription of antibiotics has been blamed for the spread of drug-resistant bacteria. Levels of triclosan have also been discovered in breast milk and in fish. The US Environmental Protection Agency registers it as a pesticide, giving it high scores as a risk to both human health and the environment. Dioxins (linked to cancer) are also formed when it is manufactured.

Parabens
Found in: Deodorants, moisturizers and toothpastes.
Purpose: Used as preservative.
Words to look out for: Methyl, butyl, ethyl and propyl paraben.

Widely used as preservatives in cosmetics, parabens may trigger irritation on sensitive skin. There is also some suggestion that parabens are oestrogen mimics or 'gender-bender' chemicals. Oestrogen mimics have been linked to breast and testicular cancer and a reduction in sperm count. Difficult to avoid, as suitable alternatives are few and far between, so minimize your exposure where possible.

Sodium lauryl sulphate/sodium laureth sulphate
Found in: About 98 per cent of all bathroom products including hand and body creams, depilatories, bubble baths, shampoos, conditioners, toothpastes, shaving creams, shower gels and facial cleansers.
Purpose: Detergent, wetting agent and emulsifier.
Words to look out for: Sodium lauryl sulphate, sodium laureth sulphate.

A commonly used shampoo and shower-gel ingredient is sodium laurel sulphate or its milder form, sodium laureth sulphate. Claims about the former's damaging health effects point to it being an allergen, with symptoms including skin and eye irritation. An American College of Toxicology study reports that sodium lauryl sulphate is safe in formulations designed for discontinuous, brief use followed by thorough rinsing from the surface of the skin but in products intended for prolonged contact with skin, concentrations should not exceed 1 per cent.

What are...gender benders?
Gender benders or hormone-disrupting compounds (HDCs) are chemicals that mimic the body's own hormones. Because the body is sensitive to minute quantities of hormones, even extremely low concentrations of HDCs can disrupt natural functions.

Choosing a natural beauty routine

If what you've discovered in your bathroom cabinet has given you pause for thought, why not consider a more natural beauty regime?

Soap

Many of the major-brand soaps contain synthetic ingredients that can irritate the skin, so look instead for natural, hand-made vegetable bars. Soap can be made from all types of oil – olive, palm, coconut, hemp – so experiment with different varieties. To avoid artificial fragrances, buy soaps that get their scent from essential oils, fruit essences and herbs. Bran, seeds and other natural exfoliators will give your skin a fresh glow.

Hair care

Look for shampoos and conditioners made from natural, organic or vegetable ingredients and use only a small amount when you wash. Choose a basic shampoo without artificial fragrance or dyes and add your own choice of essential oils – 2–3 drops per application. Use grapefruit or lemon oil for greasy hair, sandalwood or rose for dry hair, and tea tree for dandruff.

If you want to colour your hair, look for natural dyes such as henna. To lighten hair, make a chamomile infusion. Put 8 tablespoons of dried chamomile flowers in a heat-proof jug with 200ml (7fl oz) of boiling water. Leave to stand for 4 hours, strain and apply to your hair. Leave on the hair for 30 minutes and then rinse thoroughly.

Bath time

Aromatherapy bath oils are preferable to strong, detergent-based bubble baths, which can dry the skin. For a relaxing bath, mix 4–6 drops of ylang ylang, marjoram or geranium essential oil into 2 tablespoons of carrier oil (olive, almond or avocado oil are perfect) and pour into a running bath. Remember that oil can make a hard surface very slippery, so take care when getting out of the bath.

Mud baths, sea salts, milk baths and Epsom salts are also natural, relaxing and therapeutic. For a naturally fragranced bath, just scatter fresh herbs in the bathwater or hang them under the tap in a muslin bag. Try rosemary, chamomile, lavender, thyme or rose petals.

Adding a tablespoon of finely ground oatmeal to the water will cleanse and soften the skin. You'll also find a relaxing herb-bath recipe in the 'Sleep' chapter (page 114).

Toothpaste

If you are worried about chemicals, avoid any brands that contain artificial sweeteners, colours, triclosan, fluoride or sodium lauryl sulphate. There are plenty of natural-based alternatives to normal toothpaste (Green People, Kingfisher, Tom's of Maine), although you may struggle to find a brand that doesn't contain one of these ingredients.

If you are feeling brave, a traditional alternative is a paste made with 1 teaspoon of bicarbonate of soda mixed with 3 drops of peppermint or fennel essential oil and a little water.

Skin and face care

Keep your facial and skin-care routine simple with home-made or natural products where possible. Instead of creams and cleansers packed with synthetic ingredients, moisturize the body with sweet almond or avocado oil with a few drops of essential oil added. To make a sensual and nourishing body oil, mix 6 drops of jasmine essential oil with 2 tablespoons of carrier oil and massage into the skin after a warm bath.

Live yoghurt is an effective face cleanser. Simply use it in the same way you would your normal cleanser and then rinse your face with tepid water. A few drops of almond or avocado oil on a cotton-wool ball also makes a great eye make-up remover – it will even tackle waterproof mascara.

For a nourishing and sweet-smelling face pack, suitable for dry skin, mash a ripe banana with 2 tablespoons of sweet almond oil and a fresh organic egg yolk. Smear on your face and leave for 10 minutes, then rinse off with tepid water.

Lip care

For softening lip balm with a bit of zing, melt 50g (2oz) of sweet almond oil with 7g (¼oz) of beeswax in a double boiler. Remove from the heat and stir in 1 teaspoon of organic set honey. Whizz into a cream with an electric whisk and add a few drops of lemon or peppermint essential oil. Pour into an old lip-balm pot or miniature screw-top jam jar and leave to set in the fridge. This should keep for about 6 months.

Hair removal

Men should use the barber's trick of soap and a natural bristle brush for a close shave. For legs and arms, a few drops of natural oil are all you need to soften the skin and lubricate your razor. Sugaring is also a natural (but still painful!) alternative to waxing.

Nail varnish

Made from a cocktail of chemicals, nail varnish is one of the most toxic and irritant of all your cosmetics. If you can't live without shiny nails, look for toluene-free or formaldehyde-free varieties. Garden Botanika (www.gardenbotanika.com) makes a toluene- and formaldehyde-free nail varnish. Better still, natural cosmetic producers Honeybee Gardens (www.honeybeegardens.com) make fabulous non-toxic nail varnishes that contain no toluene, xylene, formaldehyde or dibutylphthalate and derive their colours from natural mineral pigments.

Deodorant

Avoid aerosol deodorants. Their use of propellants makes them an environmental no-no. There are effective natural alternatives readily available, made by companies like Avalon, but if you really can't forgo your conventional deodorant look for one that contains plant-based ingredients and is aluminium-free.

Talcum powder

Talc, or magnesium silicate, is an irritant if inhaled and possibly toxic if absorbed through the skin. Make your own deliciously scented talc by adding 10 drops of mandarin essential oil and 10 drops of orange essential oil to 6 tablespoons of cornstarch. You can store this mixture in an old talc dispenser and it will keep for 6 months.

Cotton wool and sanitary protection

Cotton is one of the most intensively grown crops and is often sprayed with numerous pesticides. Look for an organic cotton wool and choose tampons and towels that are made from 100 per cent organic material and are non-chlorine bleached. Natracare makes tampons that are 100 per cent pure organic GM-free cotton; they can be found in many supermarkets.

Sun products

It's important to use sun protection when you're out in hot weather, but most commercial sun-tan products contain preservatives, UV-blocking agents and emulsifiers that can irritate the skin. NHR Organic Oils (www.nhr.kz) has a range of highly effective chemical-free organic sun-tan lotions with sun protection factors (SPFs) of up to 24, while Neal's Yard Remedies sell a natural SPF-22 sun cream with soothing organic lavender oil and calendula extract.

Pure aloe vera is the greatest natural remedy for sunburn. Look for pure aloe vera gel (over 97 per cent aloe content) in your local healthfood store – it has been proven to promote healing and is the best way to soothe sore skin.

Perfume

If you find you're the type of person who sneezes at the slightest whiff of conventional perfume, try making your own fragrance using essential oils. There are a few essential oils that can be worn undiluted as perfumes, including lavender, jasmine, sandalwood and rose.

You can also make your own cologne by adding 18 drops of your favourite essential oil to 2 tablespoons of vodka. Store the cologne in a dark-glass perfume bottle.

CAUTION: If you are pregnant, epileptic, suffer from skin allergies or are using homeopathic treatment, consult your doctor or health practitioner before using essential oils.

Romy's five favourite essential oils

Romy Fraser understands the power of essential oils. Her innovative and highly successful natural beauty company, Neal's Yard Remedies, has been capturing the health-supporting power of plant essences for the past 20 years and putting it into gorgeous-smelling massage, bath and skin-care preparations. Each essential oil has its own delicious fragrance and wellbeing-enhancing quality, but with so many to choose from, how do you know where to start? To help you choose, here are Romy's five must-have essential oils…

- **'Lavender** is my number one oil. I take it with me everywhere. It's especially good on holiday, added to sun block or after-sun to soothe burning, and for calming itchy bites. The fragrance is simple, clean and refreshing, but also really relaxing. I put drops in the bath to help me sleep and to smell delicious, and add it to body lotion for its soothing effect. It's also great added to the final cycle when washing clothes.'
- **'Neroli** – I love this oil. Great to add a few drops into the bath for kids and so good for dry skin. It also makes any plain massage oil smell instantly wonderful. And, if I'm feeling grumpy or miserable, neroli really seems to lift my mood.'
- **'Rose** – there are times when I couldn't imagine life without this oil. A few drops added to the bath help with any hormonal problems, balancing out the extremes and leaving your body feeling both sensual and calm. I always add rose to the bath before a special night out, mixing it with some drops of frankincense and neroli. Adding 2 drops to some evening primrose oil makes a wonderful facial oil to apply before you go to bed.'
- **'Bergamot** is a beautiful and versatile oil. Its refreshing, cleansing quality means that it's great to use after a day travelling in cities, when your skin is feeling dirty and oily. A few drops added to your shampoo or conditioner are also perfect if you are suffering from an itchy or a dry scalp.'
- **'Frankincense** – my transforming oil! If I want to treat myself to some time on my own or meditate, this is the one. It's excellent to blend into a cream to help prevent wrinkles, but I also like to mix frankincense with lavender and add it to hand cream or a body lotion.'

For more information on Neal's Yard Remedies see 'Useful addresses', page 136.

PURE PAMPERING
Create your own detox home spa

Pollutants and chemicals can build up in the body, leaving you feeling sluggish and under par. Detoxing may not get rid of all these unwelcome guests, but a day spent cleansing your system with a home spa will not only help your body free itself from unwanted toxins but also leave you feeling calm and relaxed. So why not take the phone off the hook, lock the bathroom door and settle down to some serious pampering with one or more of these simple but effective treatments?

Dry skin brushing

YOU'LL NEED:
A body brush with soft, natural bristles.
TREATMENT TIME:
5 minutes.
REPEAT: Daily.

The lymph system is crucial to your body's detoxification process. Lymphatic fluid absorbs harmful toxins and transports them to your skin, liver and kidneys where they are safely eliminated. You can stimulate your lymphatic flow, and therefore speed up the detox process, by dry skin brushing. Popular in spas on the continent, this treatment not only helps you detox but also has the added bonus of improving the look, feel and tone of your skin.

Sit on the edge of a chair or bath. Starting at your feet, brush upwards with a soft, natural-bristled brush in long, firm strokes to the knee. Brush the entire bottom half of your leg and move on to the thigh and bottom area. Then, starting at your hands and working upwards again, brush your arms, shoulders and neck. Take care around delicate skin areas and always brush in one direction, towards the heart. Finish by brushing in a gentle, circular motion on your stomach, always moving clockwise. Repeat daily for best results.

Hydrotherapy

YOU'LL NEED:
A shower or bath.
TREATMENT TIME:
1 minute.
REPEAT: Daily.

Another simple way to give your lymph and blood circulation a kick-start is by finishing off any warm bath or shower with a quick blast of cold water. For the last minute of your daily shower or bath, run cold water over your body. It may not sound glamorous but it's as invigorating as going to an exclusive spa and alternating between a hot sauna and cool plunge pool.

Exfoliate

YOU'LL NEED:
A bath and an exfoliant
cream, either bought
or home-made using
1 tablespoon of sea
salt, 1 tablespoon
of honey and
2 tablespoons of
olive oil.
TREATMENT TIME:
15 minutes.
REPEAT: Weekly.

Exfoliation will give you the same benefits as dry skin brushing but the treatment also involves an exfoliant cream to buff and moisturize the skin.

Soak in the bath for ten minutes. This will gently soften any rough patches of skin. Climb out of the bath and apply exfoliating cream to your wet skin in slow, circular motions, paying special attention to any hard skin areas such as elbows or knees. Gently lower yourself back into the bath water and carry on exfoliating until the cream has washed off. When you have finished, pat yourself dry and apply a good moisturizer or home-made body oil (see page 25) to keep the skin soft and supple.

Aromatherapy bath

YOU'LL NEED:
A bath, an eggcup
of almond oil or full-fat
milk and 2 drops
each of lavender,
juniper and rosemary
essential oils. You
can also use a
good-quality over-
the-counter blend
designed to stimulate
the lymph system.
TREATMENT TIME:
15 minutes.
REPEAT: Weekly.

Aromatherapy oils don't just smell nice. Scents released by essential oils act on the hypothalamus, the part of the brain that influences your hormonal system. Different essential oils, therefore, have different effects on mood and body chemistry.

For a detoxing bath blend that will stimulate the lymph system, put 2 drops each of juniper, rosemary and lavender essential oils into an eggcup of almond oil or full-fat milk. Add the mixture while your bath is still running, step in and inhale your way to wellbeing.

CAUTION: If you are pregnant, epileptic, suffer from skin allergies or are using homeopathic treatment, consult your GP or health practitioner before using essential oils.

Epsom bath

YOU'LL NEED:
A bath, a massage
mitt or loofah glove
and 1kg (2¼lb)
of Epsom salts.
TREATMENT TIME:
15 minutes.
REPEAT:
Fortnightly.

An Epsom salts bath may not sound like the beauty treatment of your dreams, but, believe me, this is one of the most effective and enjoyable ways to relax and detox in the comfort of your own home. Epsom salts are made from magnesium, which will gently warm your muscles and soothe aching joints. The magnesium salt water will also raise your temperature and help draw out toxins from your body through perspiration.

Dissolve 1kg (2¼lb) of Epsom salts into a warm bath. Just relax for the first ten minutes of your bath, enjoying the soothing effect of the salty water. Then, taking your massage mitt or loofah glove, gently massage your entire body for five minutes.

After an Epsom salts bath you'll feel quite tired, so it's important to wrap yourself in a warm towel or dressing gown and relax. Better still, have the bath just before bedtime and you'll sleep like a baby.

CAUTION: Don't use Epsom salts if you have eczema, psoriasis or broken skin.

Body mud treatment

YOU'LL NEED:
A bath and spa body mud.
TREATMENT TIME:
20 minutes.
REPEAT: Monthly.

Spa mud is rich in nutrients, has a high mineral content, and is well known for its numerous healing and detoxification properties.

The best time for a mud bath is in the evening, just before you're ready for bed. Run a warm bath, add the mud as instructed on the packet, and relax for 20 minutes. You can splash the water on your face, but if you don't want to get your hair muddy, remember to wear a shower cap. When you've finished don't wash off the mud residue; just gently pat your skin dry and snuggle under your duvet for a good night's rest.

PURE LIVING PRIORITY
If you do only one thing...
...become a keen cosmetics label reader.

3

Eat

Imagine the choice. In front of you there are two bowls. One contains strawberries that have been intensively farmed, sprayed with pesticides and grown thousands of kilometres away. In the other are organic strawberries, free from synthetic chemicals and bought fresh from the local farmer that morning. Which bowl sounds more appealing? And, more to the point, which bowl would you give to your child for breakfast?

Put like that, it's hardly surprising that the market for organic produce has rocketed in the past few years. Barely a month goes by without a food scare hitting the headlines. Repeated mentions of pesticides, BSE, salmonella, antibiotic-laden meat, and GM ingredients have wobbled consumer trust. As a result an increasing number of people are redefining their relationship with food.

Rather than simply picking up the first frozen meal that comes to hand, many of us have rediscovered the inherent pleasure in growing and shopping for better-quality food. Farmers' markets and local delicatessens have blossomed in recent years, cooking and entertaining are new national pastimes and, most importantly of all, food lovers are supporting local, fair-trade and organic initiatives.

But what is it exactly about organic food that warrants such excitement and how does it relate to pure living? The second question is easiest to answer. If you are at all concerned about chemicals and pesticides in your daily life, food is a great place to start. Diet is one of the easiest and most pleasurable areas where you can take real steps towards greener, less toxic living.

The best way to answer the first question is to explain what's in organic food compared to non-organic food. Only when you look at the comparison can you see what all the fuss is about.

More of the good stuff

There seems to be a host of nutrients present in organic food that tend to be missing or present in lower amounts in non-organic food. Several British and American studies have shown that fruit and vegetables grown without the use of artificial chemicals often have a higher vitamin and mineral content than their conventional cousins. Research has shown, for example, that organic apples usually contain higher levels of vitamin C than intensively farmed varieties. In other food products the same has been found with minerals, including folic acid, iron and selenium. One reason for this may be that nutrients are lost when plants are forced to grow too quickly using artificial fertilizers. And many people say that most organic foods, because they're encouraged to grow at a more natural pace, have a better, more developed flavour than conventionally grown produce.

There is another group of nutrients present in plants and chemicals known as 'secondary metabolites' that include phenols, flavonoids, alkaloids and tannins. These have also been shown to be present in greater quantities in organic food. Phenols, which act as antioxidants (anti-cancer chemicals), have been shown to be more abundant in organic fruit and wine, for example. It's thought that this might be due to pesticides containing high levels of nitrogen, which destroy phenols.

The difference between organic and non-organic meat is also not just a matter of taste. Since the 1930s it has been known that the healthier the animal, the healthier the meat and produce. For example, polyunsaturated fats, which can help decrease cholesterol, are present in greater quantities in organic meat thanks to the type of feed given to the animals. In a similar way, studies on chickens have shown that those reared naturally on grass and in free-range environments produced much tastier eggs. By choosing organic animal produce, you're not just encouraging kinder living environments for animals, but often getting much better-quality food too.

EXPERT ADVICE **Antony's tips for organic meat**

According to top chef Antony Worrall Thompson, quality British meat is out there. You just have to know where to look. His experience as both a chef and a smallholder has shown him that more naturally raised animals live healthier, longer lives, eat better food and ultimately produce tastier cuts of meat. Antony has this advice for anyone considering the switch to organic meat:

- 'In my London restaurant, Notting Grill, we try to serve a different pure-breed steak every month. Look for organic beef from traditional cattle breeds such as Welsh Black, Highland and Shorthorn. For taste and texture they simply can't be matched. By buying these ancient varieties you're also helping to keep greater diversity within British farming.'

- 'Don't be too keen to look for lean beef. Organic beef is usually fattier than conventionally reared beef, which improves both the texture and taste when it comes to cooking. Ideally, beef should be gently marbled with a creamy layer of fat on the edge.'

- 'Many organic meat producers will sell directly to you either at your local farmers' market or direct from the farm. This is a great way to get good value and high-quality cuts from a reputable supplier.'

- 'Organic meat can be expensive but it's worth knowing that some cuts are pricier than others. Braising joints are proportionally cheaper than most of the other cuts, for example, so ask your butcher for advice.'

- 'Try something different. Goat, a meat eaten widely all over the world, is increasing in popularity because of its good flavour and naturally low fat content. Mutton has real depth of flavour and is delicious if cooked slowly and lovingly, while venison and wild boar offer exciting, rich alternatives to the traditional Sunday roast.'

For more information about Antony Worrall Thompson's exciting new food range, kitchen products, restaurant and latest news, visit www.awtonline.co.uk.

Less of the bad stuff

On the other side of the coin, there are countless chemicals and diseases found in conventional farming that are absent or rare in organic food.

Take pesticide residues, for instance. A 1999 report from the UK Ministry of Agriculture, Farming and Fisheries showed that about half the fresh fruit and vegetable samples tested contained pesticide residues. Safety may have been established for individual pesticides in certain circumstances but, as the Soil Association points out, 'The long-term effects of pesticide residues and the implications of "cocktail effects" on human health have not been established.' A seventeen-year study carried out at the University of Denmark, for example, has shown that women with higher-than-average levels of pesticides such as dieldrin in their bloodstream had double the risk of breast cancer. Dieldrin is now banned for use in the UK but, as with many other pesticides, persists for many years in the environment and the body.

Other studies show that pesticide residue levels are too high on some fruit and vegetables. Spinach on sale in one leading UK supermarket was discovered to have residues of the pesticide methomyl, which affects the nervous and hormonal systems, at one and a half times the safety level for adults and two and half times the limit for toddlers.

The picture is the same in other countries. A major 1998 study in the US found that 1,000,000 American children consume unsafe levels of organophosphates from the food they eat. Organophosphates have been shown to cause long-term damage to the developing brain and nervous system.

Even banned pesticides are getting through. In a recent study the UK government's Pesticide Residue Committee found that many food items, including half of all lettuces tested, were found to contain traces of pesticides that are illegal in the UK.

Organic vegetables with Rose

Rose Elliot MBE is the UK's best-loved vegetarian cookery writer. 'I've found that the more organic fruit and vegetables I use, the more I want to use. Even if they do require more washing and preparation, and sometimes look a bit more uneven (which I like), organic fruit and vegetables are a joy to use. My favourites are:

Potatoes

'With around half the main-crop and new potatoes tested by the government in 2002 showing pesticide residues, including one described by the World Health Organisation as "extremely hazardous", it's well worth buying organic. It's such a joy to know you can eat the skins of organic potatoes safely: jacket potatoes, baked with really crunchy skins, are probably my favourite "convenience" food. And then there are tiny new potatoes, boiled in their skins and tossed in melted butter and chopped fresh mint.'

Apples and pears

'When two out of every three pears and more than one in four apples have been shown to have pesticide residues, I don't feel comfortable about eating the skins unless I buy organic. Even if you can avoid pesticides a bit by peeling off the skin, who wants to? Especially as one of the pesticides found in apples has been restricted in the US to protect children's health, and a growth regulator found in pears has been described by the US Environmental Protection Agency as a "probable human carcinogen".'

Lettuces

'Leafy vegetables are particularly likely to contain pesticide residues (including illegally used pesticides which are toxic to the nervous system) and you can't get rid of them by peeling. I love to make a big bowl of salad using bronze-coloured organic oakleaf lettuce tossed in a light vinaigrette, with chopped chives from the garden. I could eat that every day – and often do, in the summer.'

continued overleaf...

Bananas

'Children love them, yet more than half of the bananas tested in 2002 contained residues, including one described by the US Environmental Protection Agency as "likely to be carcinogenic in humans". Sometimes organic bananas are a bit green, but they soon ripen up if you put them in a bowl and leave them at room temperature for a day or so. They're the best instant, portable convenience food and very versatile in the kitchen: you can make them into sandwiches, mash them into cakes, slice them and serve with curries…I like whizzing them with soya milk and frozen strawberries for a thick, creamy, iced smoothie, or dipping peeled chunks first into clear honey then into carob powder and finally into chopped nuts, and freezing to make the healthiest "choc ices" in the world.'

Oranges

'Tests have shown that 100 per cent of all soft citrus fruit contain residues including endocrine-disrupting chemicals which research has linked with declining sperm counts, and breast and testicular cancer. So buying organic seems essential if you want to avoid these. A glass of freshly squeezed orange is an instant pick-me-up – it's all that vitamin C that lifts you. Or, for a versatile salad, cut the peel off oranges and slice the flesh; then, if you want it savoury, mix with any of these: chicory, watercress, sliced mild onion, avocado; alternatively, for a sweet salad, drizzle with clear honey and a few drops of orange flower water to create an exotic, Middle Eastern flavour.'

Look out for Rose Elliot's BBC book *Fast, Fresh and Fabulous* for more fantastic vegetarian recipes and ideas.

When you buy organic you are also supporting a healthy farming system, one that ensures a high standard of animal welfare and food safety. BSE, commonly known as 'mad-cow disease', was one of the most famous farming scares to hit the headlines in recent years. Consumers were shocked to learn that cows, which are natural herbivores, were being given protein feed that contained meat from diseased animals. Organic cattle, on the other hand, are fed a natural diet with a strong emphasis on organic grass. It's no surprise, then, to find that there hasn't been a recorded case of BSE in a herd managed organically since before 1985. Other diseases, including salmonella, listeria and E. coli, which cause millions of cases of food poisoning in the UK each year, are much rarer in organic food. In fact, in 2000 the UN Food and Agriculture Organization concluded that 'organic farming potentially reduces the risk of E. coli infection'.

The routine use of antibiotics in conventional farming is also a problem.

Consuming low levels of antibiotics in food over a period of time may cause health problems, especially in children. The EU, for example, recently banned Chinese imports of shrimps and prawns following the discovery of the illegal cancer-causing antibiotic chloramphenicol.

The intensive use of antibiotics in traditional farming (to treat disease and promote growth) has led to fears that a new breed of 'superbugs' will emerge, many of which can transfer to humans and all of which are resistant to antibiotics. Salmonella resistance to antibiotics, for instance, has increased from 5 to 95 per cent in the last two decades. In the UK a House of Lords Select Committee on antibiotic resistance recently concluded that the use of antibiotics in animal feed for growth promotion should be banned. The report stated that 'we may face the dire prospect of revisiting the pre-antibiotic era. Misuse and overuse of antibiotics are now threatening to undo all their early promises and success in curing disease.' In comparison, organic farms use significantly fewer antibiotics than conventional ones.

Artificial colourings, sweeteners, flavourings and preservatives are also a 'no-no' in organic food production, which permits only a very limited number of agents. According to the UK Food Commission, consumers may be exposed to a mixture of up to 60 additives in one conventional meal, many of which are linked to a range of health problems including cancer, hyperactivity and allergic reactions. Canthaxanthin, for example, which is the colourant used to make salmon more pink, could be responsible for eye damage and the EU has called for levels to be reduced.

Another 'problem' you won't find in organic farming is genetically modified (GM) food. Although supporters of GM technology believe that it could be used to improve many aspects of modern production, such as growing drought-resistant crops, 70 per cent of the UK public remains unconvinced. At this stage too little is known about the long-term effects on human health and the world's complex ecological relationships. Even government bodies remain sceptical. In the UK in February 2003 South Gloucestershire County Council became the largest local authority to go GM-free. This means that no GM crops are to be grown on council-controlled land. Supermarkets are also taking a stand. Marks & Spencer food products are made without genetically modified ingredients or derivatives, and Waitrose's own-label and pet foods avoid the use of GM soya and maize. In response to overwhelming customer concern, Sainsbury's has also eliminated GM ingredients from all its own-brand food, pet food and dietary supplements.

Go local

If you can't find organic produce or you think it may be too expensive for your budget, your next best option is to buy local food in season. In general, locally grown produce isn't treated with as many chemicals as food grown to be exported. That's because regional produce doesn't need to be picked unripe and then treated with chemicals for a long journey and shelf life. Local food is also good for the environment (less transport, less packaging, less pollution, less waste) and the local economy (creating jobs, supporting local business, and giving farmers more for their produce). Look out for your local farmers' market – there you'll find food and drink native to your region and be able to chat to local producers about their work. In fact, these gatherings are becoming so popular, because of growing interest in local, well-made food, that the value of all food sold at UK farmers' markets in 2002 was worth a whopping £55 million.

Five easy ways to shop organic

Shopping for organic produce has never been easier. Each of the ways below is by no means exclusive. Mix and match. You could pick up your organic basics from the supermarket, get seasonal fruit and vegetables delivered to your home, explore the local farmers' market for meat and dairy produce, and then take your time choosing organic wine from an online retailer.

Box schemes

Why not get a box stuffed full of delicious organic fruit and veg delivered directly to your door? The produce is usually very fresh, seasonal and reassuringly muddy. You can also be certain that your money is going to support the local farming community. Many box schemes will also deliver meat, wine and dairy produce. The Soil Association's online Organic Directory (see www.soilassociation.org.uk) provides a list of all the box schemes in operation around Britain.

Farmers' markets

Farmers' markets, like box schemes, are booming worldwide. Shoppers love the experience of wandering around old-fashioned stalls stuffed with seasonal fare and farmers get a good price for their produce by selling direct to customers. It's not just a rural phenomenon either. Monthly gatherings are held in car parks and inner-city community centres as well as the more traditional rural locations such as fields and public open spaces. Not all food on farmers' markets is organic but local, seasonal produce is often low in pesticides and preservatives anyway. For a full list of farmers' markets across the UK, visit the National Association of Farmers' Markets website at www.farmersmarkets.net.

PURE SHOPPING
Green & Black's chocolate

Organic living is no longer the domain of the brown-rice brigade. Many of us, including chocolatiers Green & Black's, have realized that you don't have to sacrifice taste in order to take care of your wellbeing or the environment.

DID YOU KNOW...?
Of chocolate samples tested by a UK government agency,* 75 per cent contained the toxic pesticide lindane, despite its use being banned or severely restricted in nearly 40 countries.

* Working Party on Pesticides Residues Annual Report 1999.

FOR MORE INFORMATION, see 'Useful addresses', page 134.

In 1991 husband-and-wife team Craig Sams and Josephine Fairley made the world's first organic chocolate, a high-quality, bittersweet dark chocolate bar, packed with 70 per cent cocoa solids – enough to make chocolate fans sit up and take notice. The British are the world's biggest chocolate consumers, eating around 10kg (22lb) per person per year. The problem is that most of it is of low quality. Mass-market chocolate tends to have a low cocoa content, with the bulk consisting of vegetable fat or butterfat, emulsifiers, milk solids, flavourings and a large amount of sugar. Green & Black's chocolate, on the other hand, contains more cocoa solids than the majority of chocolate brands and is made with cocoa butter instead of vegetable fat. The result is 'chocolate to die for', according to the *Daily Express* newspaper.

And it's not only the chocolate that's tempting. In an industry renowned for poor wages and high pesticide use, Green & Black's is one of the only companies offering an alternative. Its farmers use no pesticides and its 'Maya Gold' bar was the first product ever to be awarded the Fairtrade mark.

Supermarkets

Supermarkets in the UK now offer an impressive range of organic essentials alongside their conventional produce. For the weekly shopper most of the leading stores have a good choice, from rice to ready meals. Sainsbury's, for example, stocks over 1000 organic products, including the world's first certified organic prawns, but other chains such as Waitrose, Marks & Spencer, Tesco, ASDA, Safeway and the Co-op also have lots to offer. The range varies, however, depending on where you live. There is also a new breed of organic supermarket, like As Nature Intended, and Fresh & Wild, which conveniently sells everything under one roof. See 'Useful addresses', pages 132 and 133, for more details.

What is...the Soil Association?

Founded in 1946, the Soil Association is the UK's leading organization for organic food and farming. Its symbol is the country's most recognizable trademark for certified organic food and wherever you see it you can be sure that your produce has met strict environmental and animal-welfare standards. As well as organic food, the Soil Association certifies health and beauty-care products, textiles, wood and paper products, restaurants and cafes.
For more information, see 'Useful addresses', page 131.

Wholefood shops

Previously seen as the bastion of the hemp-sandalled, wholefood shops have gained the recognition they deserve as reliable organic and eco-friendly stockists. These shops are especially good for dry organic goods, such as seeds, nuts, pulses and cereals but many are increasing their range to include fresh local produce, complementary medicines, household goods and organic delicatessen foods.

Online and mail order

Remote shopping is very appealing, especially for those with busy lives. Simply order your weekly shopping online or over the phone, put your feet up and smile at the thought of all those long checkout queues you've avoided. The organic sector is well represented in this area but prices, delivery options and service can vary, so shop around for the company that best suits your needs.

For a list of mail-order and online organic companies, see 'Useful addresses', pages 131–7.

Pure pampering
Detoxing smoothies and superjuices

Poisons and toxins can enter the body via food and drink as well as from your environment. Your body can detox itself naturally, but if you have been overindulging or eating badly it might be a good idea to give your system a boost. 'Superjuices' contain the most potent detoxing properties. Made from organic fresh fruit and vegetables, they will give your body a kick-start and encourage the elimination of unwanted toxins, helping to restore your inner balance.

SERVES 1

Pink grapefruit and orange

Citrus juice is perfect at breakfast time, when the body is active in its detoxification cycle. As well as the vitamins in orange juice, this drink provides you with pink grapefruit juice, which is rich in beta-carotene and bioflavonoids, particularly naringin, renowned for thinning the blood and lowering cholesterol.

3 oranges (or 300ml (½ pint) orange juice)
1 large pink grapefruit (or 300ml (½ pint) pink grapefruit juice)

Juice all the ingredients and serve immediately.

SERVES 1-2

Apple and carrot booster

Carrot juice is famous for its detoxifying properties and apple is thought to have a beneficial effect on the liver, a major detoxing organ. Pectin, which is found in apple juice, forms a gel that breaks down toxins in the intestine. This sweet and revitalizing blend of apple and carrot will aid in the elimination of excess fluid and toxins and may help ease the symptoms of a hangover.

8 medium carrots
2 apples (Cox's, Royal Gala or Braeburn)

Juice and serve immediately. You can also add a small amount of fresh root ginger to the blend, for a rejuvenating boost of flavour.

SERVES 2

Sri Lankan soother

If you've been overindulging, this sharp but refreshing drink should help relieve your misery. Recommended by well-known medical herbalist Anne McIntyre, the grapefruit and lime juices will restore depleted vitamin C levels and help your liver to metabolize toxins. The cumin not only adds a warm, spicy flavour but also enhances the detox process.

600ml (1 pint) grapefruit juice
2 teaspoons lime juice
1 teaspoon ground cumin

Blend all the ingredients and serve chilled.

SERVES 1

Beetroot blush

This is a serious power juice. Beetroot is thought to stimulate the lymphatic system, the method by which unwanted toxins are transported to your skin, liver and kidneys to be eliminated. Add to that the therapeutic effects of apple and carrot juice and you have a wonderful, health-giving body cleanser.

1 raw medium beetroot
1 apple
3 medium carrots

Juice all the ingredients and serve immediately.

SERVES 4

Banana, citrus and oat smoothie

This recipe from Champneys, one of the UK's leading health spas, takes a bit of preparation but the results are delicious. The lemon juice stimulates the liver and makes an excellent cleansing start to the day, while the yoghurt can help protect the stomach lining against irritants such as alcohol and cigarette smoke. Oats are packed with nutrients and make perfect energy food, while bananas contain vitamin B6, which is known to improve 'happy hormone' levels that are depleted if you regularly drink alcohol. Try to keep all the ingredients organic.

50g (2oz) rolled oats
100ml (3½ fl oz) skimmed milk
3 small bananas
finely grated zest and juice of 1 lemon and 1 orange
150ml (5fl oz) low-fat live yoghurt
150ml (5fl oz) low-fat fromage frais

3 tablespoons clear honey
pinch of mixed spice
8 ice cubes

Pour the milk over the oats and leave to soak in the fridge overnight. In the morning put all the ingredients, including the oats and milk, into a blender and blitz until smooth. Pass through a fine sieve and serve in ice-cold glasses.

SERVES 2

Lemon and ginger zinger

Lemon juice speeds up the elimination of fluid and toxins via your kidneys and bladder while ginger is not only stimulating and warming, but also aids digestion and is thought to have antioxidant properties. This is a delicious drink that can be served either hot as a tea or ice-cold as a thirst-quenching beverage.

25g (1oz) fresh root ginger
600ml (1 pint) water
juice of 1 lemon
honey, to sweeten

Put the ginger in a saucepan, add the water and bring to the boil. Simmer for 30 minutes. Discard the ginger, add the lemon juice to the water and sweeten to taste with honey.

PURE LIVING PRIORITY

If you do only one thing…
…put at least one organic food item in your shopping basket every time you shop.

4

Work

Working from home has some wonderful advantages. My commute involves padding down two flights of stairs, my cat dozes in the in-tray and, as my own boss, I can start, stop and take tea breaks whenever I wish. Planning to work from home, however, is more complicated than simply setting up a computer on the kitchen table. You'll need to create a home office conducive to both work and wellbeing.

The benefits of working from home far outweigh any potential problems, such as low motivation, loneliness and dealing with your own business finances. Feeling in control of your life is of great importance to physical and emotional wellbeing. Although home workers and telecommuters rarely get to pick and choose every part of their working life, the sense of independence and autonomy that comes with being self-employed is hugely rewarding.

If you do decide to work from home, whether part-time or full-time, you'll probably be spending most of the day in your office. Bearing in mind that you'll be working on average 40 hours a week in this small space, it's vital that you create a safe and healthy working environment. To do this, we need to look at the potential problems that can arise as a result of office working and simple ways to tackle them.

GETTING STARTED
How healthy is your home office?

If you work from home you probably spend as much time in your own office as you did when you were employed by a company – if not more. As an employee of an organization you were protected by strict laws governing hours, conditions and working environment. These regulations are designed to make sure your health isn't compromised by an unscrupulous boss. Now you work from home, you need to look after your most valuable asset – your health. Are you as strict with yourself as you should be? Would your home office pass a health and safety test? The following elements of office health and safety are legal requirements in the UK.

Hazardous substances

Where hazardous substances are concerned, employers must ensure that their use is necessary. They must also make certain that the recommended precautions are taken when dealing with the substances.

1. If you use them in your work, do you always use and dispose of the following hazardous substances according to manufacturers' instructions?

- Cleaning products (bleach, ammonia, solvents, degreasers and disinfectants)
  YES / NO
- Art products (lead-based inks, waterproofers, photographic chemicals, glues)
  YES / NO
- Hobby products (paints, thinners, strippers and varnish, wood preservatives, MDF sawdust)
  YES / NO
- Gardening products (pesticides, weed and insect killers, flea sprays)
  YES / NO

- Beauty products (nail-varnish remover, hairspray)
  YES / NO
- Office products (solvent-based markers, glues, spray adhesives)
  YES / NO

Health and hygiene

Employers must ensure that air-conditioning systems are properly maintained to avoid the growth of legionella bacteria, which are responsible for legionnaires' disease.

1. If you have an air-conditioning unit at home, is it properly maintained and checked?
   YES / NO

Temperature

In an office the minimum room temperature required is 16°C (61°F).

1. Is the temperature in your office 16°C (61°F) or more?
   YES / NO

Workspace

Staff who permanently occupy a workstation should be allocated a minimum of 11 cubic metres (388 cubic feet) of space. That's a cube that measures roughly 2.25m (7ft 4in) wide, 2.25m (7ft 4in) high and 2.2m (7ft 2in) deep.

1. Take a tape measure to the work space in your home office. How much space have you given yourself? Is it 11 cubic metres (388 cubic feet) or more?
   YES / NO

As well as legal requirements, health and safety regulations recommend that you do the following:

1. Do you take frequent short breaks from your computer?
   YES / NO
2. Do you sit at arm's length from your computer screen?
   YES / NO
3. Do you keep your photocopier in a different room from your office?
   YES / NO

4. Do you keep your laser printer in a different room from your office?
YES / NO

5. Do you turn off all your office equipment when not in use (standby mode counts as an appliance being switched on)?
YES /NO

6. Do you have a comfortable office chair – one that is specially designed to support your back and encourage good posture?
YES / NO

7. Is your work area arranged in order to minimize the possibility of injury through movement?
YES / NO

8. Are you subject to passive smoking?
YES / NO

9. Do you have any assistance when you need to handle or lift a heavy object?
YES/NO

N.B.
This test is not a comprehensive list of all issues surrounding health and safety in the workplace. If you are thinking of working from home or setting up your own business, visit www.hse.gov.uk for more information.

If you ticked NO in any box between 1 and 4 you need seriously to reconsider your working practices or your health may be at risk. If you have ticked NO in any box between 5 and 9 (or YES for question 8), you might want to think about changing your working practices to minimize the chances of injury, illness and discomfort. The following pages contain simple tips to help you do this.

Identifying and tackling office hazards

It's long been recognized that there are various health problems and discomforts associated with office work, especially computer-related tasks. Although there is much research still to be done, some of the health implications include visual problems, back pain, skin disorders and migraines. Fortunately, as a home worker, you have a greater amount of control over your working environment than someone working in a company office. With a few tweaks you can remove or significantly reduce most of these problems. And even if you don't work from home, many of these changes can be implemented in a commercial office without too much bother.

Eye strain and headaches

Working on your computer for more than two hours per day, or ten hours per week, is a visually demanding task with health and safety implications, according to trade unions. High-volume screen-based work puts you at risk of what's known as visual fatigue or tired eyes. This can be experienced as eye-strain, burning, sore or irritated eyes, blurred vision, contact-lens discomfort, headaches and mild nausea. Although these symptoms can be uncomfortable, research currently suggests that they are temporary with no long-lasting ill effects. Good working practices, as outlined below, should reduce most of these problems.

PURE LIVING SOLUTION: Follow the 20/20/20 rule: every 20 minutes, look at least 20 feet away for 20 seconds. Take regular breaks from your screen and do something that requires your eyes to focus elsewhere, such as looking out of the window or making a cup of tea. Provide adequate task lighting – a good desk lamp that pivots for maximum flexibility is ideal. If your font size is too small, you may be straining your eyes – increase the size of your font or consider a screen magnifier if this is the case. Place your monitor at arm's length, 60–75cm (2–2½ feet) away, to prevent headaches. Monitor screens will reduce the glare.

Neck, shoulder and back-ache

Neck, shoulder and back-ache are common complaints from people who regularly work in offices. Problems arise when you hold your muscles and limbs in one position for a long time, as you do when you are working on a computer. Bad posture, which can be exacerbated by unsuitable furniture, can also lead to muscle pain and injury.

PURE LIVING SOLUTION: Get up and stretch at regular intervals during the day. This will give your muscles a chance to move about (see 'Pure pampering: Desk-based stretches and relaxation exercises', page 58). Buy the best office chair you can afford, one that is adjustable and supports your back. If you can't get hold of a new chair, a lumbar support or rolled-up towel is a good temporary alternative. Tilting your head forward can lead to neckache, so keep the top of your monitor at eye level. This can be tricky if you have a laptop but is easily remedied with an inexpensive separate keyboard. Make sure your mouse is at the same height as your keyboard and close to hand so you don't have constantly to reach, which causes shoulder pain. To ensure good posture, keep your feet flat on the floor or use a foot rest. A document holder placed next to your monitor will stop you having to look up and down continually, and invest in a speaker phone to prevent muscle strain from cradling the phone between your neck and shoulder.

Work-related upper-limb disorder

Work-related upper-limb disorder (WRULD), or what used to be known as repetitive strain injury (RSI), has symptoms that include pain in your muscles and tendons, especially in the arms, wrists and hands. The cause is usually performing a task that involves repetitive movement, often at an awkward angle, such as typing with your wrists bent slightly upwards.

PURE LIVING SOLUTION: When typing, your wrists should be kept straight, not bent upwards (you should never use the feet on a keyboard to make it slope towards you). Striking the keys too hard, as well as typing too fast or for too long, are all recipes for WRULD. Make sure you take frequent 15–30-second typing breaks and perform a wrist stretch once an hour (see 'Pure pampering: Desk-based stretches and relaxation exercises', page 58). Think about getting a soft pad to place in front of your keyboard that will reduce the strain on your wrist. Choose a mouse of the right size and orientation – if you are left-handed, you'll need a different mouse from that supplied for right-handed users. And if you use a pen or pencil for most of your work, pick one with a comfortable grip; one that doesn't require too much pressure to hold it steady.

Office air pollution and temperature

Photocopiers and laser printers are common sources of indoor pollution in the workplace. They can emit ozone gas, which is great in the atmosphere but not in your home office (see 'What is…ozone?', page 54). In addition, toner powder for laser printers can become airborne and contribute to atmospheric contamination, particularly when cartridges are being replaced. Consider what's

PURE SHOPPING David Colwell Design

When it comes to furniture, you don't have to forfeit sleek design or back support for the sake of eco-friendly credentials. David Colwell Design specializes in steam-bent furniture which is visually stimulating, ecologically sound and wonderfully comfortable. Made from English ash, their chairs, including the office castor chair, are renowned for their strength and posture support. Companies have been so impressed that past customers include the Royal Fine Art Commission for Scotland, the Imperial War Museum and the Natural History Museum in London and the award-winning National Museum of Wales.

FOR MORE INFORMATION,
see 'Useful addresses', page 133.

With over 20 years of impeccable ecological integrity, the company is a pioneer of sustainable design and clean production. Not only does steam-bending create elegant ergonomic curves, it also seasons the timber quickly and uses a fraction of the energy of conventional methods. And, rather than import foreign woods, which is heavy on polluting fuel, David Colwell Design uses timber from local organic woodlands.

As well as being practical and eco-friendly, David Colwell Design's furniture is visually stunning and has been on show at exhibitions worldwide, including those at the Design Museum and Victoria and Albert Museum in London, the Smithsonian Institution in Washington DC and the New York International Contemporary Furniture Fair.

 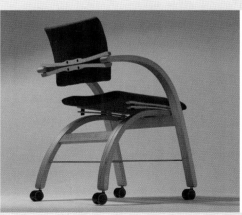 

outside your window. If you live near a busy road, it's best to keep your window closed to keep out car fumes. Temperature-wise an office colder than 16°C (61°F) will be very uncomfortable for any length of time. Keep the temperature at a pleasant, constant level.

What is...ozone?

Ozone is a gas that forms in the atmosphere. High up in the stratosphere, ozone protects us from the sun's harmful UV rays, but at ground level its presence can be harmful.

Car exhausts, factory emissions, photocopiers, laser printers and chemical solvents are some of the main sources of ground-level ozone. This makes the urban office a particular hot-spot, with workers being subjected to both indoor and outdoor sources of 'bad' ozone. Even at low levels, ground-level ozone can trigger a variety of problems including chest pains, coughing, throat irritation and nausea. It can also aggravate bronchitis, heart disease, emphysema and asthma.

PURE LIVING SOLUTION: Keep photocopiers and laser printers out of your home office, isolated in a separate room. If you haven't got space, house them in an enclosed area like a cupboard. Make sure your office is really well ventilated – keep a window open if possible, unless you live by a main road.

Clean ventilation or air-conditioning ducts thoroughly on a regular basis to remove any dust or debris, which might trigger an allergy, and check external and internal air vents to make sure your air-conditioning system is working properly. If you're not sure how to do this yourself, or your system needs to be maintained professionally, contact the manufacturer for advice.

Handle ink cartridges as little as possible, as these contain highly toxic chemicals as well as ozone, and change cartridges only in a well-ventilated environment. Follow the guidelines in the 'DIY' chapter (page 116) when you are choosing materials for your desk, flooring and room decoration to avoid further indoor pollution. Keep a few house plants in your office. Not only do they create a sense of wellbeing but they also reduce indoor air pollution (see 'Did you know...?', left).

Office supplies and hazardous substances

Paints, glues and other office supplies may contain solvents that contribute to respiratory and neurological problems. Some work-related products such as correcting fluids and markers are used by solvent abusers, who experience a dangerous high from inhaling the vapours. Craft glue, for example, contains solvents that act as neurotoxins (poisons that affect the nervous system) if inhaled. Spray adhesives are also a potential problem, and if inhaled can cause dizziness, headaches and nausea. Other hazardous substances, such as craft supplies, cleaning materials and photographic chemicals, can also result in health problems. Oil paints, for instance, can often contain cadmium, lead, chromium and other poisonous heavy metals.

PURE LIVING SOLUTION: Choose non-toxic office and hobby supplies. Look for products that are solvent-free, non-toxic or 'safe for children', as they'll also be safer for you. When using any hazardous substances, make sure you've read the manufacturer's instructions before you use or dispose of them. Use any solvent-based glue, spray adhesive or other products in a well-ventilated room.

Clutter
Do you have stacks of magazines, newspapers and books in your office waiting to be read? Are you constantly misplacing important letters and documents underneath piles of papers? Clutter in the office is not only unsightly but it could actually be affecting your performance. Excess paperwork is the scourge of many a home office, and as a result you might be finding it difficult to concentrate on important tasks and to organize your work space. At a professional level, unpaid bills, unread bank statements and unprioritized work will end up coming back to haunt you, as a home business needs to be as efficient and smooth-running as any commercial enterprise. A sloppy work environment may lead to sloppy workmanship. As for your health, excess paperwork is stressful to be around, a serious fire hazard, and collects dust (which can trigger any allergies you may have).

Electrical and magnetic fields (EMF)
There are invisible electrical and magnetic fields wherever there is electric power. Together they are called electromagnetic fields (EMFs) and they radiate from anything where an electric current flows, including all home wiring and electrical appliances. This means everything from your TV to your electric blanket emits EMFs.

For more than a decade, scientists worldwide have been trying to establish whether EMFs affect human health. For a long time it was thought that EMFs were harmless, but increasing amounts of research suggest that there could be a link between electromagnetic fields and cancer (including leukaemia), miscarriages and skin melanomas. One now-famous study carried out between 1976 and 1983 by Dr Savitz of the University of Colorado found that children

Dawna tackles the problem of paperwork

 Dawna Walter, presenter and co-author of BBC Television's *Life Laundry*, knows a thing or two about junk. Over the past decade she's helped thousands of people realize that clutter has an adverse impact on health, safety and emotional wellbeing. With excess paperwork being the single biggest contributor to cluttered environments in homes and offices, Dawna has this advice for anyone struggling to keep on top of it:

- 'Your filing cabinet, or whatever filing system you use on a day-to-day basis, should contain documents only for the last two years. Anything older should be boxed, clearly labelled and put in safe, dry storage space such as a loft or cupboard.'

- 'Create files for the most usual types of correspondence you receive. These should include individual files for each bank-account communication, credit-card statement and bill you receive on a regular basis. Next, create files for permanent documents, such as instruction manuals, guarantees, or take-away menus. Now, create files for all the other paper that is relevant in your life. For example, you might need files for paperwork about your children, or for information relating to special projects. These files should be reviewed monthly to update or discard.'

- 'Make the decision to deal with paperwork every day it enters your life. Dispose of junk mail immediately. Check and file bank statements and credit-card bills as soon as they arrive. If you find an error, it is easier to resolve if dealt with promptly.'

- 'Transfer all addresses, phone numbers and diary events you have collected on loose bits of paper into the relevant diary, address book or computer. Get rid of the scraps of paper. Remember to repeat this exercise at regular intervals in the future.'

- 'Revisit your paper-clutter hot-spots in two weeks. If you find that papers are beginning to pile up again, see if they relate to a particular area of your life. Continue monitoring your progress to make sure you don't fall into old habits.'

Extract from *The Life Laundry: How to De-junk Your Life* by Dawna Walter and Mark Franks. Copyright © Talkback Productions Limited 2002. For more ways to achieve and maintain a clutter-free home, check out Dawna's book *Life Laundry 2: How to Stay De-junked Forever*.

with cancer were 50 per cent more likely to live near high-voltage power cables, which emit a particularly strong dose of EMFs. Not everyone was convinced by Savitz's study, but it sent out a clear warning signal. Even in 2003 the US Environmental Protection Agency states: 'We lack key information necessary to make a judgement as to how far one should live from high-power transmission lines to be safe. We don't know how risky it is to actually live under transmission lines.' Many authorities are considering burying them underground.

If scientists can't decide about EMFs and power lines, they certainly can't decide whether domestic electricity and electrical appliances should be a cause for concern. Most authorities do agree, however, that frequency and nearness of exposure to EMFs are important determinants of risk – in other words, how often you use an electrical item and how close you are to it when it's in use. Most EMFs are minute, for example, once you are about 1m (3ft) away from the appliance. This makes reassuring reading as most electrical items in the house are used quickly or we don't sit too close to them.

One area of concern, however, is computer monitors. We spend a great deal of time sitting near computer screens and recent research has shown that EMFs may disrupt the body's ability to prevent the growth of human breast cancer cells. Other research, with animals, found that magnetic fields of the type emitted from computer monitors had a detrimental effect on the embryos of several species.

PURE LIVING SOLUTION: The London Hazards Centre, a UK health and safety resource, believes that until there is conclusive proof that EMFs present no risk, a precautionary approach is best. It's difficult to avoid technology in your office, so the wisest thing to do is implement some common-sense safety measures. EMFs diminish very rapidly the further away you get from an appliance, so sit well back from your computer screen. The Swedish National Institute of Occupational Health suggests that we buy low-emission VDUs, reduce the amount of time we spend in front of our computer screens, and fit VDU screens with EMF filters. Liquid crystal display screens, the type found on laptops, are also thought to be safer. To reduce the total burden of EMFs in the home office, it might also be a good idea to streamline the amount of electrical equipment you have in your office, switch from fluorescent to normal light bulbs, and turn off all equipment when it is not in use.

PURE PAMPERING Desk-based stretches and relaxation exercises

Routine office activities, such as typing or holding the phone, can cause muscle pain and discomfort, so it's important to practise a few gentle relaxing stretches at regular intervals throughout the day. These are just a few of the stretches you can perform to ease any muscle stiffness and help to avoid problems such as WRULD (see page 52) and neck pain. There are no hard-and-fast rules about how often these should be done, so simply stretch when you feel the need. The breathing exercise will also help your body to relax if you are feeling stressed out.

IMPORTANT
If you are recovering from an injury, check with your GP before embarking on any type of exercise. If you experience any discomfort while doing these exercises, stop immediately.

Back stretches
1. Stay sitting in your chair with your feet together. Gently reach down towards your feet and try to touch the floor in front of your toes. Keep your head and neck relaxed and floppy. Hold for 15 seconds and come up slowly.
2. Stand up and put your hands on your hips. Gently twist at the waist so you are stretching to look over your right shoulder. Hold for 10 seconds and repeat on the left side.
3. Stay standing up and stretch your arms above your head, thumbs touching. Lean back gently so your arms and back make a curve, as if you were going to do a back-dive. Hold for 5 seconds.

Wrist, hand and finger stretches
4. Put your palms together as if you were praying. Keeping your elbows up and palms together, move your hands downwards until you feel a mild stretch in your inner wrists. Hold for 5 seconds.
5. Buy a small foam 'stress ball' and squeeze it as hard as you can in one hand, holding for 10 seconds. Then squeeze the ball ten times in quick succession. Swap hands and repeat.

6. Splay your fingers so that all the fingers are separate and straight. Hold this stretch for 10 seconds. Then bend your fingers at the knuckles (imagine yourself saying 'Grrrr!') and hold for 10 seconds. Repeat both stretches.

Neck and shoulder stretches

7. Stand with your feet apart and shoulders relaxed. Keeping your shoulders still, tip your right ear slowly towards your right shoulder until you feel a stretch in your neck. Hold for 5 seconds. Repeat with the other shoulder.
8. Lock your fingers together behind your back, keeping your arms as straight as possible. Raise your interlocked hands until a stretch is felt in your shoulders. Hold for 10 seconds.
9. Hold your right elbow with your left hand. Look over your right shoulder and gently pull your elbow towards the opposite shoulder until a stretch is felt. Hold for 10-15 seconds. Swap hands and repeat.

Breathing exercise

10. Sit back comfortably in your chair with your arms hanging loosely by your sides. Breathe in slowly and deeply to the count of three. When you can't take in any more air, breathe out gently to the count of four. Repeat five times, taking care not to hold your breath.

Pure living priority

If you do only one thing…
…remove the photocopier from your home office space.

5

Baby

Having a baby is stressful enough without someone telling you that you're doing things the wrong way. That isn't the aim of this chapter. Its purpose is instead to draw your attention to some of the common concerns that surround babies and chemicals in the home. And to offer straightforward solutions that shouldn't affect the amount of time, money or energy you need to spend doing the difficult, rewarding and wonderful job of being a parent.

In the same way that it's important to give your baby a stimulating and loving environment, so too is it vital to provide safe, healthy surroundings. Most parents are rigorous when it comes to child locks, safety gates and keeping medicines out of reach, yet few know about the invisible danger of toxins and synthetic chemicals in everything from baby food to nursery bedding.

A child's immune system is not fully developed until the age of five, which makes the first few years of infant life a vulnerable time. Babies eat more in proportion to their body weight than adults, and have a faster respiratory rate, which makes them more likely to ingest and breathe in environmental pollutants. Milk, fruit and vegetables – a baby's staple diet – are the foods most likely to contain pesticide residues, while air-borne pollutants often collect just above floor height, exactly where babies and toddlers breathe.

A recent Greenpeace scientific study revealed that house dust contains dangerous chemicals brought into our homes via everyday products like toys, televisions, carpets and toiletries. These chemicals include akylphenols, phthalates and brominated chemicals, all of which are thought to disrupt hormones and are found in products as wide-ranging as fire retardants, plastics and cosmetics. House dust affects everyone, but this issue is especially relevant for babies and toddlers who spend most of their time crawling, sitting and playing at the level where most house dust collects – that is, on carpets and floors (see the 'DIY' chapter, page 124, for more information).

Exposure to this sort of environmental pollution, whether it's from food, air or other sources, has ramifications for health in both childhood and later life. Scientific evidence is increasingly showing a link between toxins found in the home and a wide range of problems including asthma, eczema and developmental abnormalities. Kelly Preston, spokesperson for the US Children's Health Environmental Coalition, began her campaign against toxic chemicals in the home when her two-year-old son was hospitalized after inhaling fumes from carpet-cleaning agents. 'It's not like 30 years ago, when the only way you'd get poisoned was if you accidentally swallowed something from under the sink,' she believes. 'Now it's as simple as breathing the air or eating certain foods.' So, from baby bedding and bath products to furniture and nappies, it's time to reassess what's going on in the nursery.

The great nappy debate

Nappies are among the most controversial items when it comes to health and housekeeping. My mother, who raised both her children in traditional terry nappies, recalls the whole experience as a nightmare. For her the introduction of disposables would have meant drier, happier babies and no more smelly, backbreaking nappy laundry. In recent years, however, concerns have been raised about the bleaches, perfumes and other chemicals found in disposable nappies, not to mention their poor eco-credentials. So what's a parent to do?

There's no denying that disposable nappies are handy, especially when you're out and about with the baby. But convenience always comes at a price. Disposable nappies often contain chemical additives such as bleaches, inks and perfumes that may cause skin irritation and breathing problems in babies. A recent US study, for example, found that the harsh perfumes and chemicals in disposables could trigger eye, nose and throat irritation in babies, including symptoms similar to an asthma attack. The plastic covers on these nappies may encourage nappy rash, and most disposables contain water-absorbing gels which can be toxic if they are ingested or come into contact with your baby's skin.

There's also research to suggest that disposable nappies may explain the rising incidence of male infertility and testicular cancer. German paediatricians found that throwaway nappies keep babies' bottoms too hot, which may affect the growth of infant testes.

Non-reusable nappies have also come under fire from the green movement. Disposables aren't really disposable – every one that's been thrown in a landfill still exists and won't decompose for another 200 years; when you think that worldwide parents throw away nearly 3 billion disposable nappies each year, that's a staggering amount of toxic rubbish.

The environmental cost is high, but so is the financial burden on you. On average, a baby will use 6500 nappies in its lifetime, at an estimated cost of around £2000. Compare that to the cost of cotton nappies, washed at home, which is more like £600, and you can see why some parents are switching back to cloth. And it's not only parents who are looking for alternatives. In response to the environmental and child health issues that surround disposables, many hospital maternity units have changed their ward policy to using only cotton nappies.

However, it wouldn't be fair to say that all disposable nappies are bad and all cotton nappies are good. The pesticides and other chemicals that go into growing and processing cotton mean that many cloth nappies aren't toxin-free either. What's more, the energy you'll use washing cotton nappies at home can add a significant amount to your household fuel bill. And, let's face it, there are many situations, like travelling away from home, where disposable nappies take much of the stress out of baby changing. So, when it comes to solving the great nappy debate, here are some practical suggestions to help you strike a balance between convenience, price, health and environmental responsibility.

PURE LIVING SOLUTION: Buy pre-folded cotton nappies with Velcro fastenings that are worn like a disposable; they come with biodegradable, flushable liners to capture solids and make washing easier. If you don't want the hassle of washing nappies, you can use a local nappy laundry service which still works out cheaper and greener than using only disposables (see 'Pure shopping: Cotton Bottoms', page 65)

Always wash babies' nappies in mild, non-bio washing powder. Better still, find an eco-friendly laundry detergent – these are usually made from natural, less allergenic ingredients.

Can't bear to forgo disposables entirely? Why not just use them when you're out and about, keeping baby's bottom in cotton around the house?

If you want to use disposables but are worried that your baby might be sensitive to the chemicals, look for nappies that are unbleached, unperfumed, hypo-allergenic or specially designed for sensitive skin. Avoid nappies that contain water-absorbent gels.

Look for biodegradable disposable nappies. You can buy them in many supermarkets or through green mail order/Internet companies. The Natural Baby Company sells two kinds of eco-friendly disposable nappies by mail order: Moltex, which have no added bleach, perfumes or deodorants, and Tushies, which are gel-free, perfume-free disposables with cotton and wood-pulp padding. These types of nappies are ideal for anyone who wishes to reduce the level of chemicals in contact with their baby's skin but wants the convenience of disposables.

If you can find them, 100 per cent organic cotton nappies are the most environmentally friendly option. If you opt for non-organic cotton nappies, wash them several times before your baby wears them for the first time. This should remove any residual processing chemicals. For a detailed list of all companies selling organic and traditional cotton nappies, contact the Real Nappy Association (see 'Useful addresses', page 131).

Baby toiletries

There's a plethora of baby shampoos, wipes and lotions all claiming to be kind to delicate skin. In reality most baby toiletries contain a vast range of chemicals and a key thing to remember, according to the Good Housekeeping Institute, is that you probably don't need most of them. This is especially true in the first year of your baby's life when his or her body's natural oils should be left to do their own work.

Bath time

Bath time is a favourite with many babies, but be careful about what you add to the water. Bubble bath has, for instance, been linked to urinary-tract infections in small children. When your baby is still small, stick to lukewarm water where possible, but for those situations where water alone won't suffice, avoid soaps that contain synthetic ingredients which can irritate your baby's delicate skin. Instead, look for natural, unperfumed bars made from vegetable oil. Use any soap sparingly, and if you want to buy a baby shampoo choose fragrance-free or 'no tears' varieties. Also keep an eye out for the increasing range of natural baby products, especially ones that use organic ingredients.

Lotions and creams

Unless your child suffers from especially dry skin, you shouldn't need to bother with baby lotions. If the skin is dry, try a natural alternative such as almond oil or one of the excellent natural baby creams available (see 'Useful addresses',

PURE SHOPPING Cotton Bottoms

Cotton Bottoms was founded in 1997 by husband-and-wife team Joanne and David Freer, who saw a gap in the baby market. Parents wanted the health, cost and eco-benefits of cotton nappies but were put off by the thought of washing them at home. Joanne and David realized that busy families simply didn't have time to be dealing with mountains of soiled nappies.

FOR MORE INFORMATION, see 'Useful addresses', page 133.

The solution? To sell environmentally friendly cotton nappies and provide a laundry service that takes away used nappies and replaces them with clean ones. The idea was a winner. Now, six years on, Cotton Bottoms sells more than 200,000 cotton nappies per year and is stocked in selected John Lewis, Co-op and Boots stores nationwide. The award-winning family-run business is also extending its existing nappy laundry service beyond central London, Hampshire and West Sussex to encompass Devon, Dorset, East Sussex, and north and south-east London.

But it's not just parents who are delighted with the products and services supplied by Cotton Bottoms. Many health-care professionals and day-care centres are switching to real nappies on the increasing evidence that bottoms in cotton experience fewer allergies, less nappy rash, and good postural support. A further seal of approval was given by 15 NHS hospitals, which now insist on using Cotton Bottoms on all newborns.

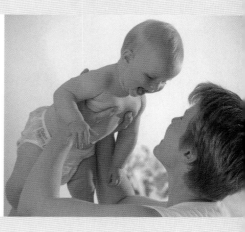

pages 129–37). Nappy rash can be a painful problem, but you can pick up simple fragrance-free barrier creams made from zinc oxide and castor oil. Letting your baby run around nappy-free for as much of the day as possible will also help prevent nappy rash.

Baby wipes

Consider what comes into contact with your baby's most intimate parts. Baby wipes are usually over-packaged and crammed with synthetic fragrance and preservatives. They also often contain alcohol, which can irritate and dry the skin. Stick to simpler alternatives such as warm water on a cotton-wool pad, or prepare a home-made gentle cleansing solution. Lynda Brown, author of *Organic Living*, suggests mixing 3½ tablespoons of distilled water, 1 tablespoon of vinegar, 2 tablespoons of aloe vera gel, 1 tablespoon of calendula oil and 1 drop each of lavender and tea tree essential oils. Stored in a dark-glass bottle, this solution will keep for up to six weeks.

Baby powder

Baby powder smells wonderful but talc has been linked to breathing problems in babies. Neal's Yard Remedies recommends making your own soothing baby powder with 3 tablespoons of cornflour, 5 drops of propolis tincture and 2 drops of Roman chamomile essential oil. Whatever powder you choose, keep it out of your child's breathing range by applying it with your hand rather than showering your baby in a cloud of white powder.

Baby toiletries and eczema

In the 1950s fewer than one in 20 British children had eczema. Now, 50 years on, almost one in five young people is affected by the skin condition at some stage in their life. Dr Michael Cork, a consultant dermatologist at Sheffield University, believes that conventional soaps, bath and shower gels and baby wipes are a huge factor in this four-fold increase.

Rising eczema rates are mirrored by increasing sales of these products. Dr Cork believes that families, especially those with a history of eczema, should look at new ways of keeping clean. 'Soaps and detergents break down the skin barrier and this effect is more pronounced in those with atopic eczema. If we do not change the increasing exposure to these environmental agents, the prevalence of atopic eczema is going to increase even further.'

The solution? Take great care when using scented soaps, bubble baths, body creams and baby wipes. Choose hypo-allergenic products, preferably as natural as possible, and always patch-test on a small area. To relieve the symptoms of eczema, one of the most talked-about discoveries is SK cream,

Jill's tips for natural baby products

Jill Barker established the popular Green Baby shop and mail-order company in north London and is an expert on the range of natural and organic products available for babies. She has this advice for any parent wanting to switch to natural baby-care products:

- 'Your new baby's skin requires very little more than water for the first few weeks. When buying baby-care products bear in mind that the skin absorbs much of what is put on it, so check the list of ingredients carefully and avoid anything artificial. If organic ingredients are used, the products do tend to work out more expensive, but remember – a little goes a long way.'
- 'Natural fibres allow your baby's skin to breathe. Conventional cotton is one of the crops most heavily treated with artificial pesticides and in some countries cotton has also been genetically engineered. Clothing made from organic cotton is free of harmful pesticides and chemicals that are often used in the processing of conventional cotton garments. By choosing organic cotton clothing you may be able to help alleviate some of the allergic and asthmatic symptoms in your child.'
- 'Most new conventional cot mattresses have been treated with fire- and water-retardant chemicals. These chemicals may cause respiratory problems and skin allergies. Natural alternatives are available and for a little more money offer more peace of mind. If you decide to buy a new conventional mattress, try to allow it to air in a well-ventilated room for several days before allowing your baby to sleep on it.'
- 'A nappy is the one item of clothing your baby spends the most time in, so it is important to choose the right type. The better choice for your baby's health and the environment is to use cloth nappies. There are plenty of varieties to choose from, and nappy laundry services in most areas of the UK. If you do choose disposables, try to use ones without chemical additives such as super-absorbent gel, chlorine bleach, lotions and perfumes.'
- 'The best baby wipe is a washable wipe made of soft organic cotton, but as this is not always practical you should try to buy wipes that do not contain alcohol, perfume or artificial ingredients.'

For more information on the Green Baby range of natural products see 'Useful addresses', page 134.

made by British organic farmers David and Margaret Evans, whose company is called Healing Products. It's never advertised, but thanks to word-of-mouth this completely natural cream is sold all over the world. You can also get a lanolin-free version for babies (see 'Useful addresses', page 134).

Baby clothes

Babygrows, vests and bootees are irresistibly cute, but your infant may be allergic to the artificial dyes, non-iron finishes or water-resistant coatings applied to many fabrics. Instead, look for baby clothes made from natural, untreated fibres such as cotton or wool. Choose organically grown fibres if possible, from companies such as Greenfibres and Green Baby, as conventional cotton and wool production often uses dangerous chemicals such as organophosphates. Organic clothing can be more expensive than conventional brands, so you might like to concentrate on the items that go directly next to the skin, such as underwear or babygrows. An economical option is to buy gently used clothing at a charity shop, as this will have had most of the chemicals washed out. It's also wise to wash brand-new clothes before bringing them in contact with newborn skin, and always use a mild, non-toxic detergent (such as Ecover) when washing your baby's clothes.

Dummies and bottles

Dummies and baby-bottle teats can be made from polyvinyl chloride (PVC). This contains phthalates, which are suspected of disrupting hormonal functions in the body (see 'Did you know...?', opposite page). Wherever possible, choose silicone or natural rubber dummies and teats.

In the US the Consumers' Union has highlighted potential problems with baby bottles. Clear, rigid, plastic bottles made of polycarbonate have been found, when heated, to leach a hormone-disrupting chemical (bisphenol-A) into baby formula at 40 times the safe limit. It's impossible to tell whether your plastic bottle is made of polycarbonate plastic just by looking at it, so the Consumers' Union advises parents to avoid clear, rigid baby bottles and opt for glass or coloured, opaque varieties instead. Green Baby and Spirit of Nature both sell glass baby bottles in the UK.

Baby food and milk

Babies and toddlers are voracious eaters, consuming vast quantities of fruits, juice, milk and vegetables every day. Most conventionally grown produce contains chemical residues, so it's important to buy organic food as babies 'are less able to detoxify most pesticides than adults', says Dr Philip Landrigan, director of community and environmental medicine at the Mount Sinai School

DID YOU KNOW...?
Disruptive or difficult behaviour in young and older children can be a sign of clinical hyperactivity. Diet seems to play a major role in this disorder as certain common chemical food additives, such as the colouring sunshine yellow (E110), have adverse effects on some children. The Hyperactive Children's Support Group (www.hacsg.org.uk) has produced a very helpful booklet on hyperactivity and diet – see their website for more details or call 01243 551313.

PVC contains chemical additives that can present a threat to human health. These include phthalates, used to soften plastic, which have been linked to reproductive problems in humans. As a precaution while more scientific work is done, the US Consumer Product Safety Commission (CPSC) has requested that manufacturers remove phthalates from soft rattles and teethers and has also asked the industry to find a substitute for phthalates in other products intended for children under three years old that are likely to be sucked or chewed. Similar bans are in various stages of effect throughout the EU and some toy manufacturers, such as LEGO and Brio, have already stopped using PVC in their products.

of Medicine in New York. A study reported recently by scientists at the University of Washington also found that children fed predominantly organic produce and juice had only one-sixth the level of pesticides in their urine than children who ate conventionally farmed foods. 'This justifies the importance of an organic diet, that organic foods lower a child's exposure,' says Dr John Wargo, a specialist in risk analysis at Yale. If studies are finding out that pesticide residues have even the potential to cause harm to health, as is suggested by the growing evidence, it's surely important not to gamble with our children's health in this way. By buying organic food, you will also avoid many of the problems associated with artificial food additives and hyperactivity (see 'Did you know…?', opposite page).

It's also well-known that breast is best when it comes to feeding your baby, but many studies have shown that toxins and unwanted chemicals can be passed from mother to baby through breast milk. If you are a nursing mum it's advisable to eat organic foods and avoid alcohol for both your health and the health of your baby. Or, if you've found breast feeding isn't the right option for you and your baby, there are a number of very good organic infant milks and follow-on formulas available.

For more information about the benefits of organic food, see the 'Eat' chapter, page 32. For organic baby food manufacturers see 'Useful addresses', page 129–37.

Baby toys

Soft toys can harbour allergy-causing dust mites, pollen and pet dander as well as containing harsh dyes and residual chemicals from the manufacturing process. An easy solution to both these problems is to buy washable, organic-cotton soft toys and put them in the washing machine once a week at water temperatures of 60°C (140°F). Soft toys that can't be washed can be placed in a plastic bag and left in the freezer for three to four hours to kill off any dust mites.

Many baby and toddler toys are made from soft PVC plastic, including rubber ducks, teething rings and squeaky animals. Young children are notorious for sucking and chewing their toys and there is real concern that dangerous chemicals, found in PVC, are leaching into babies' mouths and damaging their health (see 'Did you know…?', left). Greenpeace is campaigning for manufacturers to remove PVC from such toys, but in the meantime choose non-PVC alternatives such as natural wooden toys and teething rings. Make sure, however, that the paints used to decorate them are non-toxic and, above all, look for solid, well-made toys that will be durable and imaginative enough to sustain your baby through his or her early years.

GETTING STARTED
Designing a naturally healthy nursery

From birth young children are building their immune system, so it's important to create a safe, healthy and stimulating environment. There's a strong temptation to fill a new nursery with brand-new carpets, bedding, toys and clothes, as well as giving the room a lick of paint. Unfortunately, you might be unwittingly exposing your newborn to harmful chemicals from these various products. The DIY chapter (page 116) gives more details about the various pros and cons associated with do-it-yourself and decorating products, but here's a quick checklist specifically designed for naturally healthy nurseries, inspired by David Pearson's brilliant *The Natural House Book*:

1. Paints should be lead-free and low in volatile organic compounds (VOCs). Use natural paints if possible (see page 118).
2. Furniture, toys and clothes should meet approved safety standards and be made from natural materials where possible.
3. Reduce exposure to electromagnetic frequencies (EMFs) by keeping the cot at least 1.2m (4ft) away from any working electrical appliances and arranging the furniture so that your baby is not sleeping close to wiring circuits in walls. You could also consider fitting a 'demand switch' in the nursery which would cut off the electricity at night. See the 'Work' and 'Sleep' chapters (pages 55 and 110) for more information on EMFs.
4. Your baby should have a sturdy cot, with no sharp edges, preferably made from untreated wood finished with beeswax. Bars should not be more than 37–50mm (1½–2in) apart and the drop side must have a locking device. Some models can be converted to a toddler's or full-size bed as baby grows, saving you money in the long run.
5. Choose 100 per cent natural fabrics and fillings, preferably organic, for the mattress and bedding (see 'Sleep', page 106, for more details). Avoid plastic undersheets as they trap moisture and can contain harmful chemicals.

6. Synthetic carpets can contribute to indoor air pollution, so look into low chemical alternatives currently being developed by the carpet industry or choose a natural floor covering such as wood, wool, jute, sisal or coir.

7. A nursery should be a place of rest and relaxation, so avoid harsh primary colours or busy wallpaper. Choose harmonious, neutral shades instead and liven up the space with creative and inspiring pictures. Young children love pictures of the natural world, so put these up alongside drawings and paintings done by your child.

8. Avoid fluorescent lights. Use good-quality lighting and design for plenty of natural sunlight.

9. Newborns cannot regulate their temperature so it's important to keep the room at a pleasant, consistent 18–20°C (64–68°F). Fit radiator covers to prevent burns.

PURE LIVING PRIORITY

If you do only one thing…
…switch to chemical-free nappies.

6

Clean

Cleaning's a dirty job but someone's got to do it. There's satisfaction to be gained from the end results of a good spring clean, but on the whole housework is a time-consuming yet necessary chore. It's no wonder, then, that manufacturers have spent years, and millions of pounds, developing household products that claim to do the job in half the time or produce cleaner, sparkling homes with minimum effort. But are these 'wonder products' really making our homes safer, healthier places to inhabit?

To help sell cleaning products, advertisements constantly warn us of the 'hidden dangers' lurking in our homes. As a result, housework can sometimes feel like an epic struggle against the forces of dirt, bacteria, grease and stubborn stains. However, recent research suggests that over-the-top household hygiene may be doing more harm than good.

The hygiene hypothesis

A growing number of scientists believe that exposing children to a wide range of microbes (microscopic organisms, usually bacteria) is vital to the development of a healthy immune system. 'By stamping out bugs and parasites with better sanitation and housework, vaccination and antibiotics, we may be weakening some parts of our children's immunity, leaving other parts unchecked and overeager,' explains Dr Graham Easton, presenter of BBC Radio 4's medical programme *Case Notes*. 'The immune system is then primed to see harmless things like dust and pollen as dangerous invaders, leading to allergy, asthma and possibly even other immune diseases, such as arthritis or diabetes.'

Research backs up this hypothesis. In the *Journal of Clinical and Experimental Allergy* Swiss researchers reported that hay fever was less common in farm children (who are exposed to 'dirtier' environments) than in urban children or rural children who didn't live on farms.

Scientists also discovered that children raised in large families had fewer allergies than children born into small families, the theory being that exposure to the germs by older siblings protected the younger children from any future allergies.

Polluting the planet

As well as posing a problem when it comes to allergies, modern cleaning products contribute to environmental pollution. Many household cleaners, when washed down our plugholes and drains, harm the delicate ecosystem that exists in rivers and waterways. Surfactants, which cut through grease and dirt, damage living organisms such as frogspawn, while phosphates from household cleaners can cause algae blooms that kill other plants and water life. Bleaches undermine the bacterial action that helps break down sewage in sewage plants, and optical brighteners, used to make your whites whiter, can be poisonous to fish.

Some manufacturers are changing their policies and attempting to minimize the environmental harm done by their products. Other companies, such as Ecover, Bio-D and Clear Spring, for example, have created effective yet eco-friendly cleaning products, designed to be kind both to you and the planet. With formulas being developed and perfected on a continual basis, opting for an eco-friendly alternative doesn't have to mean choosing a drop in cleaning performance.

PURE SHOPPING Natural Collection

Modern consumers don't need more guilt. At least that's what Jo and Julian Spector, founders of the hugely successful mail order eco-business the Natural Collection, believe. Their mission is simply to show consumers that we can make a better world if given choice, convenience and good information.

FOR MORE INFORMATION, see 'Useful addresses', page 136.

From toilet cleaner to candles and bed linen to bath oil, Jo and Julian have spent the last three years developing an exciting range of eclectic, contemporary and highly desirable home and garden wares, carefully chosen to inspire a sustainable future. Their natural, practical and beautiful products have shown that you can shop responsibly without having to compromise your lifestyle – the ultimate goal of today's conscientious consumer.

Nowadays environmentally friendly shopping isn't just acceptable – it's the epitome of chic. Consumers are becoming more savvy about the contents of their shopping basket, so the Natural Collection constantly looks for products that are good value for money, don't exploit the environment or people, and are made of recycled or natural materials.

From fair trade to FSC-certified wood, many eco-issues were completely unknown to suppliers and manufacturers when the business first started in 1999. Jo's and Julian's persistence, combined with the enthusiasm of Natural Collection customers, proved that there'll always be a market for ethical, healthy and eco-friendly goods.

According to the American Association of Poison Control Centers, 53 per cent of all poison exposures occur in children under the age of six. The most common forms of poison for that age group are cosmetics and personal-care products (13.3 per cent), cleaning substances (10.7 per cent), painkillers (7.6 per cent) and poisonous plants (6.9 per cent).

Accidental poisonings

As a very young child I accidentally drank a bottle of liquid furniture polish, thinking it was milk. Luckily the contents weren't too toxic and the poisons unit at our local hospital reassured my frantic parents that I'd had a lucky escape. Other parents aren't so fortunate and every year millions of children are accidentally poisoned by a household product. In 1997, for example, the National Safe Kids Campaign estimated that over 1.1 million American children under five were accidentally poisoned. In this age group over half the poisonings were as a result of children getting their hands on common household items – including cleaning supplies and household pesticides. Drain cleaners, for example, often contain lye (sodium hydroxide), which can cause severe burns and is potentially fatal if ingested. With these kinds of risks in mind, it seems sensible to reassess how many toxic household products you really need in the home, especially when there are natural and safer alternatives now available.

Everything under the kitchen sink

You may not have children, but there are still many good reasons not to go overboard with conventional household cleaners and other products. Health and environmental organizations have expressed serious concerns about the short- and long-term effects of substances found in cleaning materials. In particular, both WWF and Greenpeace have highlighted 'persistent toxic chemicals'. These chemicals don't degrade easily in the environment, gather in the body's tissues over a period of time (a process called bio-accumulation) and in some cases can be passed to babies via breast milk. They also become more concentrated over time and are toxic to health. Unfortunately, conventional cleaning products often contain a wide variety of such chemicals, alongside other equally toxic substances. Here are some key toxins that might be lurking under your kitchen sink:

Artificial musks

Used as a cheap fragrance in many household products from fabric conditioner to air fresheners, artificial musks can be absorbed through inhalation or via skin contact. These chemicals have been shown to build up in body fat and in breast milk and some are known to disrupt the human hormone system by mimicking female hormones. Artificial musks include: musk xylene, which is known to cause cancer in mice and is listed by European governments as a priority for elimination; and musk ambrette, a known neuro-toxin that can also cause testicular atrophy. Many supermarkets are now phasing out artificial musks from their own-brand products. In the meantime, why not use essential oils or real flowers to give you a beautiful, naturally scented home instead? In the 'Relax' chapter (page 96), floral designer Paula Pryke has some wonderful suggestions for using flowers to create room fragrance.

Tetrachloroethylene

According to the Agency for Toxic Substances and Disease Registry (ATSDR), tetrachloroethylene is a chemical used for dry-cleaning and degreasing. Exposure (particularly in closed, poorly ventilated areas) can cause dizziness, headache, sleepiness, skin irritation, confusion and nausea. It can also result in liver and kidney damage and may be toxic to unborn animals and humans. The US Department of Health and Human Services (DHHS) has determined that tetrachloroethylene may reasonably be anticipated to be a carcinogen. The amounts given off by freshly dry-cleaned clothes are likely to be minimal, but make sure you thoroughly air any dry-cleaned fabric before putting it back in your room.

Para-dichlorobenzene

Found in air fresheners, toilet-bowl fresheners and mothballs, para-dichlorobenzene (P-DCB), if inhaled in high concentrations, can cause headache, nausea and confusion. It's also extremely toxic, a central-nervous-system depressant, a kidney and liver poison, and bio-accumulative. P-DCB is banned in California.

Methylene chloride

Used in certain aerosol and pesticide products, spray shoe polish, water repellents, car cleaners and other household products, methylene chloride can cause dizziness, eye irritation, nausea and 'drunkenness' if inhaled. In humans, direct skin contact with methylene chloride causes intense burning and redness of the skin. The International Agency for Research on Cancer (IARC) has classified methylene chloride as 'possibly carcinogenic to humans'. The US Environmental Protection Agency has determined that methylene chloride is a probable human carcinogen.

Phthalates

Used for a wide variety of purposes, including as a carrier for fragrance in bathroom cleaners, phthalates bio-accumulate and animal tests suggest they may cause birth defects and liver damage. See the 'Baby' chapter (page 60) for more information on phthalates.

Chlorine and sodium hypochlorite

Chlorine and its derivative sodium hypochlorite are present in a number of household cleaners. Chlorine is found in disinfectants and bleaches, for example, and can damage skin and eyes. Its fumes irritate the lungs, especially if you have an existing condition such as asthma or emphysema. Chlorine is also very toxic and combines with other organic matter to form organophosphates, which persist in the environment and the human body. Sodium hypochlorite, used in bleach, gives off highly irritating toxic fumes that can damage the eyes, nose and lungs. Ingesting even a small amount of household bleach will cause gastrointestinal irritation; larger amounts or industrial-strength bleach may cause potentially fatal corrosive injuries to the mouth, throat, oesophagus (gullet) and stomach.

Phenol

Found in polish, disinfectant and air fresheners, phenols can trigger skin rashes and may cause convulsions if swallowed. They are also suspected of causing respiratory damage.

Ammonia

Ammonia is present in many household products from scouring powder to metal polish and window cleaner, and even low levels of this substance in the air may harm asthma suffers and other sensitive individuals. Ingesting even small amounts of ammonia may cause burns to your mouth and throat, and, if dropped on the skin, ammonia will burn if not quickly washed off.

Diethyltoluamide

Diethyltoluamide (DEET) is found in commercial insect repellents. This potent substance is irritating to the skin and respiratory tract. In sensitive individuals DEET may cause allergic dermatitis and has also been implicated in seizures in children. The Children's Health Environmental Coalition (www.checnet.org) notes that DEET can cross the placenta and expose babies in the womb. It goes on to say that 'while there is no evidence of health effects resulting from exposure during the second and third trimesters, pregnant women should avoid the use of DEET during their first trimester'. Canada is phasing out insect repellents that contain more than 30 per cent DEET.

Triclosan and other anti-bacterials

Found in multi-surface cleaners, hand-washes and disinfectants, anti-bacterial agents in cleaning products are suspected of causing anti-microbial resistance. They can also bio-accumulate and have been discovered in breast milk and in fish. Some European governments have issued press statements discouraging their use in household and personal-hygiene products.

GETTING STARTED
The naturally clean home

Bearing in mind the environmental and health concerns that surround conventional cleaning products, it might be time to replace your store of synthetic sprays, polishes and gels with something altogether more natural. It might sound impractical, but natural products such as lemon juice are not only very effective as household cleaners, but they're also less toxic, readily available and inexpensive. The five main natural cleaning ingredients you'll need are:

White distilled vinegar
White vinegar is acidic, which means it can neutralize alkaline substances such as limescale. It is also an effective disinfectant, anti-fungal agent and degreaser. Freely available.

Bicarbonate of soda
Also known as baking soda. A slightly alkaline mineral used for gentle non-abrasive cleaning and deodorizing. Found in all supermarkets.

Washing soda
Used to be the most common household cleaning product. A relative of bicarbonate of soda, washing soda (sodium carbonate) is more strongly alkaline and can cut through grease, as well as deodorize. It may be used also to soften water, clean tiles, remove stains and clean bathrooms. Found in most supermarket laundry sections or at the chemist's.

Borax
This is an alkaline mineral, in powder form, which can be found in many supermarket laundry sections or at your local chemist or hardware shop. Used for cleaning, softening water, stain removal, disinfecting, and deodorizing.

Lemon juice
A natural bleach and fabric whitener. Also an effective deodorizer, degreaser and disinfectant. Freely available.

NOTE: You'll also need a few plastic spray bottles and some labels.

All of these ingredients, especially borax and washing soda, are much better for you and the environment. You should, however, always wear rubber gloves when doing household chores (even with natural products) as strong alkaline or acid solutions can irritate and dry the skin. Always keep cleaning products out of reach of young children.

Once you have these five main store-cupboard ingredients, you can create almost any household cleaning product. Some of the following recipes also use an extra component, such as lavender essential oil, to give a pleasant smell or as an active ingredient.

Kitchen

Oven cleaner: Mix 300ml (½ pint) of bicarbonate of soda with a little water to make a loose paste. Spread inside the oven, leave for a few hours to soften any dried-on material, then rinse thoroughly.

Disinfectant: Use a 1:3 solution of lemon juice and warm water. Apply to surfaces with a damp cloth and dry with paper towels to avoid residual stickiness. The US Environmental Protection Agency also recommends plain soap as a perfectly adequate disinfectant.

Deodorizer: For smelly refrigerators place half a lemon, with the cut side dipped in salt, on the middle shelf. For chopping boards, wipe the surface with half a cut lemon.

Window cleaner: Use a 1:3 solution of white vinegar and hot water, plus the juice of a lemon. Spray on to dirty windows, mirrors or tiles and remove with paper towels (or newspaper for best results).

Limescale remover: Fill your kettle with an equal-parts solution of white vinegar and water. Leave overnight and then rinse. Also works on toilet bowls.

Drain cleaner: Pour 300ml (½ pint) of bicarbonate of soda down the drain, followed by 1 litre (1½ pints) of boiling water. Quickly follow with 300ml (½ pint) of white vinegar. The chemical reaction will cause the soda to bubble and foam inside the pipes.

Bathroom

Anti-bacterial bath scourer: Mix 300ml (½ pint) of borax with 300ml (½ pint) of salt and 2 tablespoons of finely ground dried rosemary or lavender. Use like an ordinary powder scourer and rinse thoroughly.

Mould and mildew remover: Use a solution of 1:3 borax and water. Spray on the affected area, leave for 10 minutes and scrub clean.

Laundry

Stain remover: To get rid of stubborn stains, pre-soak clothes in a solution of warm water and washing crystals or borax.

Laundry whitener: Add 150ml (5 fl oz) of lemon juice to the rinse cycle. Dry the clothes in the sun for an even whiter finish.

Fabric softener: Add 50g (2oz) of washing soda to your wash cycle.

Linen spray: Take 15 drops of lavender or rose essential oil and mix it with 25ml (1fl oz) of vodka. Leave for 24 hours and then add 300ml (½ pint) of distilled water. Pour into a spray bottle.

Mothballs: Place a muslin sachet filled with cedar chips fragranced with 15 drops of cedarwood essential oil in your wardrobe or drawers. You can buy cedar chips from a wood merchant or find them ready bagged at www.onceatree.co.uk. Alternatively, try a sachet or bunch of dried lavender.

Living room

Air freshener: Mix 1 teaspoon of your favourite essential oil with 250ml (8fl oz) of water. Store in a spray bottle.

Room fragrance: Use pot-pourri, dried or fresh herbs or fresh flowers. See Paula Pryke's wonderful suggestions for flowers to fragrance the home in the 'Relax' chapter, page 96.

Furniture polish: Melt 100g (4oz) grated beeswax and 300ml (½ pint) turpentine in a bowl over simmering water (turpentine is highly flammable, so be careful). Add a few drops of lavender essential oil, pour into a jar and leave to set. Rub on to furniture with a soft rag, leave to dry, and buff with a clean cloth.

Wood-floor cleaner: Use a solution of 300ml (½ pint) of white vinegar in a bucket of warm water.

Silver polish: Place your tarnished silver in a pan with a few strips of aluminium foil in the bottom. Add 1 tablespoon of salt and 1 tablespoon of bicarbonate of soda to the pan and add enough water to cover the silverware. Leave for a few hours, rinse the silver well and dry. The tarnish is removed by a process called electrolysis.

IMPORTANT: You might not be able to find natural substitutes for all your household cleaning products. If you have to use a conventional product, and you have young children in the house, the UK National Poisons Information Service has this advice:

- Select products with child-resistant closures.
- Keep the products in locked cabinets out of reach and sight of children.
- Return the products to safe storage immediately after use.
- Store cleaning and DIY products and food in separate areas.
- Keep products in their original containers. Never put them into food or beverage containers. Don't turn your back on a child when a product is within reach. If the phone or doorbell rings, take the child with you.
- Don't allow anyone to bring industrial or workplace products for use in the home – they may be 'stronger' and more dangerous.

PURE LIVING PRIORITY

If you do only one thing…
…swap at least one of your conventional products for a natural cleaner.

7

Relax

Many of us feel out of tune with our living spaces. Our homes don't quite work for us and yet we struggle to put our finger on the problem. We buy a new piece of furniture or technology, hoping that it will redress the imbalance, but fail to see that the solution lies in the basics of a healthy and comfortable home. Light, colour, warmth, sound and scent – get these five fundamentals right and you'll have a home that not only looks fantastic but will also calm your mood, help you relax and improve your wellbeing.

The preceding chapters have concentrated largely on pollutants in the home and their detrimental effect on your wellbeing. Not having a place to unwind may seem a less immediate threat to health than chemical toxins, but the reality is that many common ailments – from stress to depression – are exacerbated by lack of relaxation and down-time. It seems so ironic that people spend hundreds of pounds a year on yoga classes, meditation and stress management, yet then come home to a soulless, uncomfortable living space where they never feel truly at ease. But what differentiates a home that comforts the soul from a house that drains the spirit and damages your wellbeing?

Light

Fundamental to any home is the importance of natural light. Daylight and wellbeing go hand in hand; our body clock is designed to follow its rhythms. At sunrise, natural light lifts the spirits and energizes us; at sunset, it has the power to make us feel reflective and serene. Sunlight also triggers bodily reactions, increasing our production of serotonin. As well as controlling mood, libido and sleep patterns, serotonin can also help to counteract depression and make us feel cheerful.

Yet 90 per cent of the population spends 90 per cent of its time indoors. We've divorced ourselves from the physiological and emotional benefits of natural light. We wake up in the dark, work in light-starved buildings and then arrive home to spend the evening immersed in artificial light. It's not surprising, then, that increasing numbers of people complain of low-level depression and Seasonal Affective Disorder.

What is...Seasonal Affective Disorder?

Seasonal Affective Disorder (SAD) is a form of depression that affects around 500,000 people in the UK during the winter months. Shorter daylight hours and less exposure to sunlight trigger a chemical imbalance in the brain, causing severe sufferers to feel depressed, lethargic and even suicidal. Other people suffer a milder version that has been dubbed the 'winter blues'. (For more information visit the SAD Association website, www.sada.org.uk.)

What's wrong with artificial lighting?

Artificial lighting imparts a wonderful ambience to the home – it can add drama or cosiness to an otherwise ordinary room. It helps us perform tasks, highlights favourite pictures or becomes a focal point in itself. In terms of serotonin levels, however, domestic artificial lighting doesn't even come close to improving our wellbeing.

Light is measured in units called 'lux' – one lux being the amount of light from one candle. Outdoor levels start at around 10,000 lux on a grey day and can soar to 80,000 in glorious sunshine. In comparison, average indoor artificial light levels are just 300 lux, so it's obvious why a gloomy house can have a direct effect on your emotional and physical health.

Bring me sunshine

Unless you have a very sympathetic boss, changing your office environment to bring in more natural light simply isn't realistic. However, we can certainly encourage more natural light into our home life. This is done in four main ways: by using living spaces according to how much sunlight they receive; by opening out internal space; by boosting the amount of light coming into the home; and by using reflected light.

Orientation: The sun travels around your house, from east to west, so it makes good sense to allocate rooms according to how much natural light they receive. To get the most from natural daylight, have bedrooms and breakfast rooms facing sunrise (east), kitchens/living rooms/work spaces/conservatories facing south, and evening rooms or storage spaces, where it doesn't matter how much light you get, to the north.

Opening up: You can also increase light in a dark house by adding transparency between rooms. Glass bricks can open out a space that would otherwise be darkened by a solid wall. French doors, Japanese paper screens and open-plan living also make the most of natural light, allowing it to flow uninterrupted through a space.

Outside in: Basement flats in particular can be depressingly dull, but there are ways to encourage more light in. Paint the wall or patio area outside your basement window white to reflect more light into the room. Be creative with water features, which can also reflect light back up into a dull room, as can light-coloured foliage.

Think about adding extra windows to your existing home. Convert small windows into French windows for a wonderful boost, or introduce clerestories, high but small windows that allow privacy while casting shafts of light across a room. Adding a bay window, skylight or tube lights (which channel daylight from your roof) will also brighten any interior. The king of natural light-spaces is, of course, the conservatory. This can be a real asset, adding significant amounts of light, solar gain (heat received through windows) and even monetary value to your home.

Off the shelf: If you can't face even minor building work, you can buy accessories that will transform a light-poor house. Reflect light back into a room with strategically placed large mirrors and invest in white or cream furnishings and fabrics. Keep window treatments to a minimum. Heavy curtains will drain precious light, so use shutters and sheer fabrics instead. If you can't bear to part with your drapes, make sure you draw them well back in the daytime. Use paint colours that contain lots of white and keep window ledges and rooms clutter-free.

Colour

People often find that they hate a particular room in their house. One day they pick up a paintbrush, try a different colour on the walls, and suddenly the room is their new favourite space. Colour can have such a profound effect on mood and wellbeing: get it right and the walls seem to sing with harmony; get it wrong and no amount of knick-knacks or new furniture will make it feel better.

Research into the psychology of colour has proved that different colours elicit different responses in humans. Leading colour psychologist Angela Wright explains why: 'It is Nature's own powerful signalling system…the colours of our environment affect our behaviour and mood. When yellow daffodils, bluebells and colourful crocuses appear, we immediately begin to feel livelier; but when grey skies and rain or snow surround us, we instinctively draw in and tend to hibernate…The colours of the interior environment wherein we live or work affect us in just the same way as those in the natural world always did.'

But not only does colour influence us on an emotional level, it actually affects us physically too. All colours form part of an electromagnetic spectrum and each colour vibrates at a different wavelength. Angela goes on to explain, 'When light strikes the eye, the different wavelengths do so in different ways; the eye constantly adjusts and long-wave colours require the most adjustment. In the retina they are converted to electrical impulses that pass to the hypothalamus, the part of the brain that governs our hormones and endocrine system. Thus colour sets up complex physiological reactions, which in turn evoke a psychological response.' So we actually physically experience colours – different colours evoke different responses, having the ability to energize, soothe or depress us.

GETTING STARTED
Is your wall colour making you blue?

Not sure whether you've cracked the colour code? The following simple advice will help you establish whether you've picked the right shade for the right room.

White

Not strictly a colour, white imparts a sense of purity and hygiene. A little white can add elegance and highlight details; too much and your house will feel cold and sterile. Pure white can be difficult to live with, so stick to light neutrals and naturals for large areas. Off-whites and calming creams add a real feeling of natural light and a heightened sense of space. Great for any room in the house.

Black

This has the opposite effect of white – it makes spaces feel smaller. Not a good colour for walls: it will make your home dark, oppressive and deeply depressing. However, used judiciously (especially next to white), black can look extremely sophisticated and convey a sense of seriousness. Great for architectural detailing, such as wrought ironwork or front doors.

Red

Attention-grabbing, energetic and stimulating, red can actually raise your blood pressure and get your pulse racing. One of the strongest colours in the spectrum, red attracts the eye and appears to be closer than it is. Use only in rooms where you want people to feel energized and talkative, such as a dining room. Can appear aggressive or lively, depending on the context.

Brown

Warm and comforting, with associations of earth and natural wood, the colour brown is one with which humans feel at home. Not a 'show-off' colour like red, brown is quietly reassuring and calming. Use light shades, such as cappuccino, for large wall areas and keep dark brown for details and woodwork. Mid-brown is best enjoyed not as a paint, but from natural sources such as stripped wood and hardwood flooring.

Orange

Another cheerful and vibrant colour, orange encourages passion and vitality and is thought to aid digestion. Sensual, fun and zesty, it is the colour often associated with Mediterranean interiors. As with red, keep orange to socializing, chatty spaces, such as the kitchen.

Yellow

Reminding us of sunshine, yellow lifts our spirits and stimulates happy emotions. It's a confident colour and needs to be used in areas where you want to feel bursting with energy, such as dining rooms, morning rooms and kitchens. Not a relaxing colour, yellow is best kept away from bedrooms and living rooms. The wrong shade can apparently make you feel anxious.

Green

A calming, restful and healing colour that suits most rooms in the home, green sits in the middle of the colour spectrum and is thought to encourage feelings of nature, balance and harmony. We instinctively feel reassured by this colour – it connects us with the outside world – but too much green can be overbearing and make you feel torpid. Looks great with crisp white.

Blue

The right shades of blue, the world's most popular colour, can aid concentration and calm the mind. A great colour for 'thinking' spaces, such as a home office. Its association with the sky and water means that we connect blue with tranquillity and open spaces, so it's also perfect for relaxing areas such as the bedroom and the living room. Colour therapists recommend blue if we are feeling under stress, but the wrong shade or too much blue can make you feel cold and unhappy.

Purple

In many Eastern cultures, purple is the colour of spirituality and meditation. In the Western world it has connotations of royalty and luxury. Physically and emotionally, lighter shades of purple such as lilac make us feel calm, so use them in areas where you need a retreat – like the bathroom, nursery or bedroom. Use darker shades for accents rather than large areas as too much dark purple can seem oppressive.

Pink

Perceived as a 'girlie' colour, pink has associations of love, nurturing and physical comfort. Used in light shades, pink can be very soothing, and in deeper shades it can inject a sense of passion.

Pure shopping
Nutshell Natural Paints

Want colour on your walls but don't want the chemicals? Nutshell Natural Paints offers the perfect alternative to conventional household paints. Nutshell was originally set up in 1990 by creative arts practitioner Eilla Goldhahn, after she spotted a gap in the UK market for eco-friendly paints. Eilla opened her first shop in Totnes, Devon, and being located in a tourist town proved a bonus as visitors quickly spread the word about her original and beautiful paints.

FOR MORE INFORMATION see 'Useful addresses', page 136.

What had originally been born out of environmental concerns soon turned into a vibrant commercial venture, helped along by a resurgence of public interest in traditional paints. Concerned about the risks associated with some of the chemicals used in paints, many people were keen to find a safer alternative. So, using natural materials, Nutshell paints were created to give the great results decorators have come to expect without exposing them to harmful chemicals.

The Nutshell range includes two types of emulsion, earth and mineral pigments, and wood treatments, all of which conform to strict ethical, eco- and health standards. Products are made using locally sourced ingredients where possible, packaging is simple and often recycled, and everything can be ordered online.

Warmth

Alongside natural light and the right colour, you also need warmth to feel relaxed. Our bodies feel comfortable in rooms at 18–25°C (64–77°F), yet many of us live in countries that regularly fall way below these temperatures. A cold living space not only feels uncomfortable, but can lead to loss of concentration and fatigue as a result of the body overworking to keep warm. It's vital, therefore, to keep a comfortable living temperature that isn't at the mercy of cold extremes.

For most of us, this means having central heating or dressing more warmly. The latter is better for the environment, uses less fuel and money, and discourages other household 'guests' such as dust mites from making themselves at home. However, walking around a cold house with five jumpers on isn't always practical or desirable, so if we do turn to central heating we need to make sure we get the most from it. If you sandwich your radiator between the wall and the sofa, you're wasting valuable heat. Place radiators underneath windows, where the warm air hits the cold air coming from the window and is circulated around the room. Make sure your living room, and the rest of the house, is well insulated so that you're not wasting heat or money. If you're buying a new house or renovating an old one, you might want to look into underfloor heating, which provides wonderful background warmth and usually costs less money to run.

A warming focal point

With the advent of central heating we always have a reliable background temperature. What it doesn't provide is a focal point. Your central heating may be warming your cockles, but without a fireplace or hearth a living room can lack the comfort factor. Staring into the flames of a crackling fire not only acts as a kind of meditation but also seems to fulfil a primal instinct in all of us, reminding us of our ancient past and connecting us with the elements.

An open fire is the ultimate tool for relaxation. Many people choose 'flame-effect' gas fires, for their cleanness and convenience, but nothing really compares to the delight of a real wood fire. As Terence Conran puts it, 'A fire without companionable sound is a fire that warms the room but not the soul.' Look into the practicality of at least one open fire (with a fireguard) in your home. Wood-burning stoves, for example, are environmentally sound and give off very few emissions of smoke and particulates (both outside and into your living room). They're also more eco-friendly than fires powered by natural gas, oil, coal and electricity from fossil fuels. So not only do you get clean air, you get a clear conscience too.

What is…carbon monoxide poisoning?

Carbon monoxide is a highly poisonous gas produced when you burn fossil fuels (including coal, wood and natural gas) without sufficient air. This usually happens when a gas appliance is faulty or an air vent or chimney becomes blocked. You can't see it, smell it or taste it, but carbon monoxide is potentially fatal if it escapes into your home.

If you are suffering from persistent headaches, sickness, extreme tiredness, dizziness or confusion, especially when your gas boiler, cooker, fire or water heater is in use, you may be suffering from carbon monoxide poisoning. Stop using the appliance immediately. Ventilate the house and call Gas Emergency Services on 0800 111 999. Visit www.house.co.uk/safety for more information.

Scent

It seems absurd that people use chemical-laden air fresheners to disguise bad smells in their home. Not only do they fail to get rid of offending odours, but air fresheners spray potentially harmful chemicals into the air you breathe. A nice-smelling room, however, is one of life's little pleasures, and can greatly enhance the enjoyment of your home, so what's the alternative?

The best solution is to add scent to your home with naturally fragranced candles, essential oils, herbs and real flowers. In her beautiful book *The Naturally Scented Home*, Julia Bird explains the growing trend for natural home fragrances: 'Indulging our sense of smell has a powerfully therapeutic effect, intensifying our enjoyment of everything we do. A bath scented with favourite essential oils becomes an oasis of calm; a glass of wine sipped on a summer's evening surrounded by the heady sweetness of jasmine…Even listening to music has a new intensity when you're relaxing in a darkened room filled with the subtle aromas of scented candles or incense.'

Modern homes are often too well sealed, leaving no opportunity for clean air to circulate. Make sure fresh air flows though your house by throwing open a window or two on a daily basis. Banish smoking from your home; tobacco smoke lingers for days and can make your house smell stale and unpleasant, not to mention the health effects of passive smoking (see 'Did You Know…?', left).

Nature's fragrances

Bring naturally good smells into your home, with one or a combination of the following:

- Fresh flowers and herbs
- Candles scented with essential oils
- Home-made pot-pourri
- Essential oils – in baths, inhalations, room sprays and oil burners
- Citrus peel
- Spices
- Incense
- Natural cleaning products (see the 'Clean' chapter, page 72)
- Linen water
- Herb pillows and sachets
- Scented smoke (place a handful of pine cones or rosemary stems on to an open fire)
- Aromatic foods (baking bread, cooking with vanilla or chocolate)

For more tips on how to create a naturally fragranced home, see Paula Pryke's 'Expert advice', overleaf.

Sound

Light, colour, warmth and scent. But what effect does sound have on your wellbeing? Exposure to noise pollution has more serious consequences than just feeling annoyed with your neighbours. Numerous studies have shown that exposure to unwanted sound (the definition of 'noise') can lead to high blood pressure, heart disease, inability to concentrate, long-term memory problems, stress, depression and in some cases violent behaviour. And yet, despite all these health problems associated with noise, according to government figures 32 million people in the UK suffer in silence (or not, in this case).

External noise pollution can have a number of origins. Noisy neighbours are now the greatest source of noise nuisance and public complaint. Roads, aircraft flight paths, businesses and organized events are also common culprits. Within the home, families can create their own cacophony with shouting, arguing, loud music and noisy appliances. It's not realistic to expect monastic silence in the home, and indeed a total absence of noise can be equally stressful and unnerving, but if you think the noise level in your house might be a cause for concern there are a number of things you can do to reduce its impact.

Paula's floral scented home

Paula Pryke is one of the world's most famous and well-respected florists. She's been described as 'the most brilliant florist in London', and her cutting-edge designs have been featured in leading magazines and television programmes worldwide. Not only does Paula understand the visual impact of flowers, but much of her work also involves using their natural fragrance to make a statement. Here are her ten favourite flowers for a naturally fragranced home:

Lily of the Valley

'I love to have fragrant Lily of the Valley on my bedside or dressing table. Although not a long-lasting flower, this is my favourite scent of all as it reminds me of my great aunts and of their wonderful scented cottage gardens.'

Sweet peas

'Originally summer blooms, these delightful flowers are now available from spring to autumn and have a light, delicate scent. Commercially grown sweet peas will last around six or seven days, whereas garden-cut sweet peas, which are far more pungent in scent, last only about three or four.'

Hyacinths

'Long-lasting and heavily scented, hyacinths are great value. They look beautiful planted in pots or as a cut flower and I love to use them in the bathroom where the heady scent is just divine for a relaxing bathtime! A little too overpowering in the bedroom or the kitchen, but perfect for hallways.'

Stocks

'These summer flowers have a fresh scent when first cut, but they are related to the cabbage family so can turn rather smelly at the end of their life. It's well worth having a vase full of these beautiful blooms on a summer evening, but remember that they'll only be good for around three or four days.'

Herbs

'I love to have a jug of mixed herbs in my kitchen, especially the combination of mint and dill. There are many flowering varieties of herbs which can be decorative as well as fragrant. Use a little bay to bulk out the vase and a touch of rosemary and you have a great "tussie mussie", very reminiscent of the type used in medieval times to ward off bad luck.'

Gardenias

'These delightful plants are rarely sold as a cut flower in the UK. If I am feeling really decadent I love to cut off their creamy and glorious flower heads and float them in finger bowls along my dining table. I have arranged so many of these blooms for weddings that they remind me of romance and give a real sense of occasion.'

Jasmine

'This is just divine as a plant for hallways or stairs and I love to use this plant in my own home in the wintertime, especially around Christmas. Jasmine also reminds me of holidays and I find its scent very soothing and restful as it always evokes happy memories.'

Freesias

'One of the staples of the scented-flower kingdom, freesias are available throughout the year and are a long-lasting cut flower. Buy them in tight bud and enjoy for at least five days, or maybe even seven if you buy the longer-stemmed varieties.'

Roses

'Garden roses are quite simply heavenly, but sadly very short-lived. There are some commercial roses that have great scents, such as 'Extase', but in the main you need to grow your own garden varieties to experience the real magic of roses. The fragrance of these flowers is another that transports me back to my childhood.'

Lilies

'The elegant and wonderfully fragranced lily is an excellent all-year-round option and great for hallways where the scent can waft throughout the whole house. The classic "Longiflorum" lily is always in style, but for me the sweet scent of the pink "Stargazer" family lilies will always remind me of my wedding day.'

Look out for Paula's latest books *Wedding Flowers* and *Classic Paula Pryke* or visit www.paula-pryke-flowers.com for more information about her shops, delivery service, and internationally acclaimed Flower School courses. See 'Useful addresses', page 136, for the full address.

Inside the home

Think about the way rooms are allocated in your house. Are noisy rooms next to quiet spaces? Can this be changed? For example, can you set up a room in the basement or attic, where older children can play their music without deafening the rest of the family? Does the TV room need to be next to a bedroom? Can the washing machine or tumble drier be heard through the nursery floor?

Noise travels through walls and floors, so check whether you've insulated these areas properly. Wooden floors look great, but bare floorboards can be very noisy for whoever's living below. Stick to bare floorboards on the ground floor only. If you want wooden floors upstairs, you'll probably have to put new floorboards on top of the existing ones to ensure decent draught and sound insulation. Natural carpet, underlay, rugs and any kind of extra floor covering will also deaden noise. If sound is coming through a particular wall, the quickest trick is to place a wardrobe full of clothes next to it. If you want something a bit more substantial, fitted wardrobes and storage, tongue-and-groove panelling or a second plasterboard wall will also reduce any noise coming from a neighbouring room.

Soft furnishings, too, can help to soften any unwanted noise created within a home. Minimalist interiors look fabulous, but noise echoes around empty spaces and bounces off hard surfaces. Think about softening the acoustics with strategically placed cushions, throws and wall-hangings, but make sure they are all washable to avoid the problem of dust mites.

Outside the home

If noise is coming from outside traffic or other external sources, check that your windows are glazed properly. Double and triple glazing is much quieter than single glass. Heavy curtains can also help to deaden sound coming through a window, but they can collect dust and darken a room. Consider fitting wooden shutters.

Soft landscaping outside the window can also reduce the amount of sound bounced into your home. Garden walls, fences, thick foliage, trees and earth mounding reflect traffic noise away.

If you have noisy neighbours, the best thing you can do is approach them calmly about the situation. Most neighbours will be totally unaware of the upset their noise is causing and will be only too happy to turn things down. If you don't have any luck, however, you may want to contact the Environmental Health Department of your local council. You'll also find sound solutions to unwanted noise on the National Society for Clean Air and Environmental Protection website (www.nsca.org.uk).

If you are just about to move house, do some detective work to make sure you're not moving into a noisy area. Check with the local council's Planning Department that you're not about to buy a house under a flight path or that the volume of road or rail traffic isn't likely to increase dramatically. Visit the potential property at different times of the day – a property may be much noisier in the evening than in the daytime. Talk to neighbours to find out about any problems specific to that street. And don't assume, if you are buying a new home, that it will have good sound insulation. In 1998 the Buildings Research Establishment estimated that 40 per cent of floors and 25 per cent of walls between new dwellings had sub-standard insulation.

Using sound to relax

Once you've banished unwanted noise, you can bring in other sounds to create a soothing, restful atmosphere in your home and garden. Different people find different sounds relaxing, but most find these pleasantly calming:

- Birdsong
- Trickling water (you can buy indoor and outdoor water features)
- Wind chimes
- Softly ticking and chiming clocks
- A cat purring
- Soft singing and chanting
- Soothing music (whether it's classical, jazz, ambient house, piano)
- Rustling grasses and leaves.

PURE LIVING PRIORITY

If you do only one thing…
…encourage as much natural light into your home as possible.

8

Sleep

We are a nation suffering from chronic sleep loss. Of all visits to family doctors 15 per cent are about sleep problems, and most of us are getting around an hour less than we really need. Work worries, family crises, money – these problems will keep most of us awake from time to time, but if you're consistently struggling to get a good night's rest it might be time to reassess your sleeping environment. Is your mattress old or uncomfortable? Have you recently repainted your room? Do you have wall-to-wall carpets? Believe it or not, your choice of bedroom furnishings could be stopping you getting the deep sleep you need.

Counting sheep

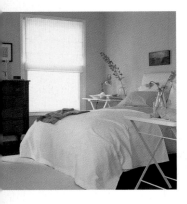

What's the problem? We all miss a night's sleep once in a while and wake up with few ill-effects. Repeated sleepless nights, however, can be devastating for your health and wellbeing. Depression, tiredness, mood swings and inability to concentrate or remember are common side effects of insomnia. Lack of sleep can lead to a tendency to pick up recurrent infections, such as colds or sore throats, because your immune system is impaired. More worryingly, chronic sleeplessness also significantly increases your chances of having a car accident or injuring yourself at work or in the home. Each year in the USA, for example, driver sleepiness is the primary cause of 100,000 vehicle accidents attended by the police, and results in 71,000 injuries and 1500 deaths.

And it's not just adults who are missing out. Around 60 per cent of children in the UK are not getting enough sleep, according to new research. Professor Jim Horne, an expert in sleep deprivation at Loughborough University, is worried that 'bedrooms are changing from places of rest and tranquillity to places where there are lots of things to keep children awake, such as computers and televisions'. Not only does this leave kids tired and irritable the next day, but continuous sleep deprivation may also harm neurological development and can contribute to behavioural problems including attention deficit hyperactivity disorder (ADHD).

Just how much sleep do we need? The widespread consensus is that an average person needs between seven and nine hours. Some people manage quite happily on less sleep than that, others need more. Elderly people often sleep for only five hours a night and supplement that with catnaps during the day. People who are unwell, on the other hand, often increase their sleep requirements. A common-sense approach is best. If you feel recharged after a night's sleep, there's no need to worry. If, however, you wake up every morning feeling unrefreshed, it's time to take action.

DID YOU KNOW...?
In a 2002 survey carried out by the National Sleep Foundation, almost 75 per cent of all adults reported having insomnia more than once a week.

The healthy bedroom

To ensure a good night's rest, it's vital that your bedroom and its contents provide a healthy and harmonious sleeping space. An important factor in creating this is keeping your bedroom free from harmful chemicals, whether they come from synthetic carpets or recently painted walls. If any member of your family is asthmatic a healthy bedroom is even more important, as dust mites, pet hair and other problems can trigger allergic reactions that interfere with sleep. Other factors such as temperature, light, noise and exposure to electromagnetic frequencies (EMFs) could also be keeping your bedroom from being a place of tranquillity and restfulness.

GETTING STARTED
Are you getting a good night's sleep?

If your room isn't the sleeping sanctuary that it should be, why not use this simple self test to help you identify and tackle any potential problems? Go into your bedroom, taking this book with you, and look around the room to see if you can spot any problem areas. Use these questions to help you, making a note of all the times you answer 'yes'.

The bed
1. Have you owned your mattress for more than ten years? YES / NO
2. Is the mattress made from synthetic foam? YES / NO
3. Is the base of the bed solid – that is, not slatted? YES / NO
4. Does the bed have a padded headboard? YES / NO
5. Does the bed have a fabric hanging or canopy? YES / NO

If you've answered 'yes' to any of these questions, turn to 'The bed' on page 106.

Bedding
1. Is your duvet or pillow made from synthetic materials – for example, is it polyester-filled? YES / NO
2. Are your sheets, pillowcases and duvet covers made from synthetic materials (for instance, polycotton) or bleached/dyed cotton? YES / NO
3. Is any of your bed linen 'easy-care' or 'non-iron'? YES / NO
4. Do you wash your bed linen less than once a week? YES / NO
5. Do you let your pets sleep on your bed? YES / NO

If you've answered 'yes' to any of these questions, turn to 'Bedding' on page 107.

Furniture

1. Do you have MDF or other particle-board bedroom furniture – for example, fitted wardrobes? YES / NO
2. Does the room have too much bedroom furniture? YES / NO
3. Is any of your bedroom furniture particularly ornate? YES / NO
4. Is it difficult to clean under any of your bedroom furniture? YES / NO

If you've answered 'yes' to any of these questions, turn to 'Furniture' on page 109.

Windows

1. Is your window closed most of the time? YES / NO
2. Do you have curtains? YES / NO
3. If so, are your curtains 'dry-clean' only? YES / NO
4. Is the room too light at night or too gloomy in the morning? YES / NO

If you've answered 'yes' to any of these questions, turn to 'Windows' on page 109.

Walls

1. Have you repainted your room recently? YES / NO
2. Do you have vinyl wallpaper? YES / NO
3. Is your wallpaper textured? YES / NO
4. Are the walls showing any sign of damp or mould? YES / NO
5. Are you unhappy with the colour/pattern on your walls? YES / NO

If you've answered 'yes' to any of these questions, turn to 'Walls' on page 109.

Electricity

1. Do you have an electric blanket? YES / NO
2. Do you have an electric clock, TV, radio or cordless phone on your bedside table? YES / NO
3. Is your bed near an electric storage heater? YES / NO
4. Do you leave appliances plugged in during the night? YES / NO
5. Do you sleep near high-voltage incoming cables? YES / NO

If you've answered 'yes' to any of these questions, turn to 'Electricity' on page 110.

Noise

1. Does your partner snore? YES/NO
2. Is your house next to a busy road? YES / NO
3. Is your house under a flight path? YES / NO
4. Can you hear your neighbours next door? YES / NO
5. Are the walls and floors in your own house particularly thin? YES / NO

If you've answered 'yes' to any of these questions, turn to 'Noise' on page 112.

Bedtime routine

1. Do you ever bring homework or office work into the bedroom?
   YES / NO
2. Is there a TV in your bedroom? YES / NO
3. Do you drink tea, coffee, hot chocolate or cola before bedtime? YES / NO
4. Do you eat dinner late (after 8 p.m.)…? YES / NO
5. …or early (before 5 p.m.)? YES / NO
6. Do you come home from work and go straight to bed? YES / NO
7. Do you ever find it difficult to switch off from the day's events? YES / NO

If you've answered 'yes' to any of these questions, turn to 'Bedtime routine' on page 112.

The bed

According to the Sleep Council (www.sleepcouncil.org.uk), it's important to replace your bed every eight to ten years. This is because old mattresses have lost their shape, leading to back problems and disturbed sleep. Research carried out by the UK Sleep Assessment and Advisory Service (SAAS), for example, found that people with uncomfortable beds sleep on average one hour less each night than those with comfortable beds.

When you sleep your body sheds heat, moisture and a plentiful supply of dead skin flakes. House-dust mites love this environment and old mattresses can harbour up to 2 million of these allergy-causing pests. As a result, asthmatics and other people with breathing problems may find their symptoms get worse at night, while eczema sufferers become prone to itching if they come into contact with the mite allergen, both of which will lead to a disturbed night's rest.

Chemical vapours may also be affecting your sleep. Poor-quality mattresses are made from synthetic foam, which can contain formaldehyde and other potentially toxic substances (see 'Fire retardants and health', below). These chemicals can leach out in vapour form for years after manufacture and may cause allergic reactions (such as breathing difficulties and headaches) that prevent you from sleeping properly.

Fire retardants and health

Polybrominated diphenyl ethers (PBDEs) are used as fire retardants in many household items including mattresses. These chemicals reduce the spread of fire but, after studies showed that PBDEs also disrupt brain development in animals and bio-accumulate in human bodies, the EU chose to ban them.

Several dozen flame-retarding compounds other than PBDEs exist, some of which pose less risk to health. However, for a totally natural and fire-safe option, look for a chemical-free mattress from eco-companies such as Greenfibres or Healthy House (www.healthy-house.co.uk). These conform to strict safety standards by having a very thick layer of cotton or pure new wool added, which acts as a natural fire retardant.

PURE LIVING SOLUTION: Large beds have been shown to aid a more restful night's sleep. Buy the biggest you can afford. You'll also need to buy the correct support, comfort and firmness for your weight – a bed that's too hard or soft can lead to postural problems and sleepless nights.

Invest in a naturally filled mattress made from materials such as coir, latex, cotton or pure new wool. Make sure the mattress cover is also made from natural materials. Change your mattress every eight to ten years, unless it's designed to last longer. If you're on a tight budget, a natural fibre-filled futon is a good, inexpensive alternative.

If you suffer from allergies, cover your mattress with a breathable anti-mite barrier cover (which you can wipe down or wash regularly). Remember that padded headboards and fabric canopies may look plush but they also make great dust traps. Opt for a simple, wooden-framed bed instead, preferably with a natural finish (see the 'DIY' chapter, page 116, for more information). You'll also need to ensure that the bed base is slatted, not solid, to encourage free movement of air and prevent a build-up of mite-friendly heat and moisture.

Bedding

House-dust mites and synthetic chemicals also pose a problem when it comes to bedding. Some people are intolerant to the fibres in synthetic fabrics (such as polycotton or polyester), especially those suffering from eczema, while others are irritated by the dyes found in most conventional bedding. Crease-resistant and 'non-iron' sheets have often been treated with formaldehyde and this is a chemical known to cause skin irritation.

Linen, cotton and flannel are more comfortable, but many 'natural' fabrics are awash with chemicals from the bleaching, dyeing and fireproofing process, none of which you want against your skin for eight hours a day.

PURE LIVING SOLUTION: Look for unbleached, undyed organic cotton or linen sheets and bedding, and consider other natural fabrics such as silk, cashmere, wool and hemp. If you can't find unbleached sheets, look for bedding bleached with hydrogen peroxide rather than chlorine. When you buy any type of new sheets, make sure you wash them thoroughly before you use them.

Look for feather, organic cotton or kapok-filled duvets and pillows – these natural fillings breathe better than synthetic alternatives and they're also kinder to the environment.

If you suffer from allergies, you'll also need to cover your pillow and duvet with breathable anti-mite barrier covers. Wash your bedding weekly, at a temperature of at least 56°C (133°F) to kill any dust mites. And although it's lovely having your pet sleeping on your bed, animal hair and dander may trigger allergies and prevent you getting a good night's sleep. Keep pets out of your sleeping space if you have asthma or breathing difficulties.

Many people are ditching their duvets and rediscovering the joys of soft, wool blankets and throws. For the ultimate in luxurious but eco-friendly bedding, layer the bed with crisp cotton sheets, topped with organic wool blankets and a hand-made quilt.

Pure shopping Greenfibres

How can you run a successful business and tell your customers to consume less, not more? Easily, if you are William and Gabriela Lana, co-founders of the eco-textile company Greenfibres.

FOR MORE INFORMATION
see 'Useful addresses', page 134.

Concerned about the woeful eco-credentials of conventional fabric production, William and Gabriela set about researching and creating a healthy, responsible and sustainable alternative. Starting with a mail-order business in London in 1997, they soon moved Greenfibres down to Totnes, in Devon, and opened their first shop selling goods and garments made from organic cotton, organic linen, hemp, organic wool, and untreated silk.

Greenfibres customers can expect high-quality products that are stylish, healthy and sustainable, from blankets and bedding to knickers and nightwear. Goods have to be certified organic whenever possible; made in environmentally responsible ways; receive no or minimal treatment or processing and be produced under fair working conditions. Not an easy task when every item from mattresses to baby mittens also has to look good, feel good and work well.

But customers love the products and enjoy making a difference by how they spend their money. 'Unlike many other companies we do not sell products that make you younger, smarter or more popular,' say the Lanas. 'We're simply here to help you find the best ecological alternatives to many everyday products – enabling you to make responsible and healthy consumption choices.'

Furniture

Much of today's bedroom furniture consists of built-in wardrobes and storage. These are usually made from fibreboard such as MDF, and may emit chemical vapours that pollute the bedroom and act as an irritant (see 'DIY', page 121, for more information). Dust is also a potent source of allergic triggers including dust mites, pollen and mould, and can be found in any cluttered or over-stuffed bedrooms.

PURE LIVING SOLUTION: Keep bedroom furniture to a minimum and choose furniture with smooth surfaces and clean lines, which makes them easier to dust. Buy movable furniture so you can easily clean behind or under it, and avoid fibreboard furniture – choose pieces made from natural wood or formaldehyde-free MDF instead. Varnish can also emit toxic vapours, so look out for furniture that's either unfinished or sealed with beeswax or natural wood oil instead.

Windows

Your windows can have a profound affect on your ability to sleep. Too much light at night and you'll find your sleep is disrupted; too little light in the morning and it'll be difficult to wake up. Heavy curtains are the solution for many people, but these bring their own set of problems, including dust and dry-cleaning chemicals.

PURE LIVING SOLUTION: 'Dry-clean only' curtains not only collect dust but can also emit dangerous fumes after they've come back from the dry cleaner's. Opt for roller blinds or shutters instead, as these will block out unwanted light but are easier to dust. If you do want curtains, buy cotton drapes that can be washed at high temperatures.

Reduce the humidity in your bedroom by leaving a window open – mites love high humidity, as do moulds. Persistently high humidity also encourages the emission of chemicals from products in the home (such as painted walls or synthetic carpets – see 'DIY', page 116, for more information).

Consider a sleep mask if your bedroom never gets completely dark at night and dip into the 'Relax' chapter (page 84) for more ways to make the most of dawn light in your bedroom.

Walls

As you'll find out in the next chapter, many paints, varnishes and vinyl wallpapers emit toxic fumes that act as irritants, causing symptoms that include sneezing, coughing and itchy eyes.

PURE LIVING SOLUTION: If any of these symptoms has been keeping you awake and you've just redecorated your bedroom, you may want to sleep somewhere else and ventilate the room until the 'fresh' paint smell has disappeared. Choose natural paints or those with a low VOC content (see the 'DIY' chapter, page 118) and avoid sleeping in a freshly painted or wallpapered room. For allergy sufferers, textured wallpaper can act as a dust trap, so avoid it altogether.

If you have black mould patches on your walls, you've probably got damp. Mould spores can also trigger sneezing, blocked sinuses and conjunctivitis, so find the source and eliminate the problem as soon as possible.

The colour of the bedroom walls can actually affect your ability to relax and drift off to sleep. Use the quick guide in the 'Relax' chapter (pages 89–91) to help you choose a soothing colour.

Electricity

Research has yet to prove either way whether electromagnetic fields (EMFs) cause health problems (see the 'Work' chapter, pages 55 and 57, for a more detailed discussion). Prudent avoidance is probably the best strategy here. Maury M. Breecher MPH and Shirley Linde PhD, in their book *Healthy Homes in a Toxic World*, advise that:

- Bedside appliances (such as phones, stereos, fans, electric clocks) should be at least 75cm (2½ft) away from your head.
- You should unplug electric blankets before getting into bed (research has shown that children whose mothers used electric blankets during their pregnancy were 30 per cent more likely to develop cancer).
- Don't place your bed within 1m (3ft) of an electric space heater.
- Don't place cots or beds on the other side of walls where TVs, video monitors, fridges, washing machines, hairdryers or electric space heaters are located – magnetic fields can penetrate walls.
- Make sure the main electrical line connecting your house to the outside electrical network doesn't enter your home within a couple of metres of bedrooms.

You may also want to switch off and unplug appliances at night and use battery-operated or wind-up technology for radios and alarm clocks.

Expert Advice · Linda's perfect bedroom

 As an interior designer for numerous TV shows (including the BBC's *Changing Rooms*), private homes and major corporations, Linda Barker has created hundreds, if not thousands, of gorgeous room schemes. But, given the choice, what would Britain's best-loved interior designer choose for her own perfect bedroom?

'The bedroom, because it's private, is a forgotten space in the house and one that people often don't get right. Unlike kitchens or living rooms, which are "show-off" communal spaces, bedrooms tend to get ignored, and yet they're one of the most important rooms in the home.'

'Your bedroom can impart a real sense of wellbeing. It has the ability to empower, invigorate, relax – whatever you want. Personally I like bedrooms to be light and airy. I prefer blues, creams, naturals and sometimes a few greens: what I would call a "spring palette". Duck-egg blue is my favourite bedroom colour; it's calming and restful, and can soften an otherwise minimal space. I also like my bedroom to be full of natural light, to give me a real boost of energy first thing in the morning.'

'A bedroom should feel friendly, comfortable and safe. I love the "pared-down" look for most of the house, but prefer to have a softer, more relaxed feel to the bedroom. To add a human dimension, I use plenty of cushions, rugs and accessories, and don't skimp with bedlinen. High-quality, tactile, natural fabrics such as silk, cotton, linen and wool have an intrinsic beauty and integrity which make me feel connected to nature, so I use them as much as possible. A thinnish duvet with blankets and throws gives a wonderful, cosy feel to the bed.'

'Lighting is also really important in the bedroom. It's vital to have total flexibility, so have a range of options: a main light with a dimmer switch, bedside lamps, and candles placed strategically to create interesting and relaxing pockets of light. Then, I use scented candles and aromatherapy oils to add the finishing touch to my very own sleeping sanctuary. Sweet dreams!'

Linda Barker is the author of a number of books on interior design, including *Changing Rooms: Finishing Touches*, published by BBC Books.

Noise

One of the most common reasons for a poor night's sleep, noise can come from any number of sources. If unwanted sound is troubling you, the 'Relax' chapter (page 95) has many ways to reduce the impact of noise in the home. If snoring is the problem, talk to your doctor or try one of the many over-the-counter treatments such as nasal strips, homeopathic drops or herbal mouth sprays. One of the most common causes of snoring is being overweight. Shedding a few pounds may solve the problem but if you've tried that and it hasn't worked, or weight isn't a relevant factor, there are other possible solutions. You might want to ask your dentist about dental snoring devices or consider minor surgery; especially if the problem is caused by nasal polyps, enlarged adenoids or a deviated septum (the British Snoring and Sleep Apnoea Association – www.britishsnoring.com – has more information on all types of snoring remedies). Failing that, there's no shame in choosing to sleep in separate rooms – the tension caused by a snoring partner is a far worse strain on any relationship. A 2001 Snoreeze Census, for example, revealed that almost half of the 1000 couples blamed their partner's snoring for rows.

Bedtime routine

Your bedtime routine might be affecting your ability to doze off and stay asleep.

PURE LIVING SOLUTION: Make sure you unwind before bedtime. Listen to soothing music, take a warm aromatherapy bath, or read a gentle book. Avoid watching TV in bed as this can over-stimulate your brain just when your body is telling you it needs a rest.

Eat too early and a grumbling tummy will keep you awake. Eat too late and your digestive system will be in full swing just when your body is trying to slow down for sleep. Ideally, eat a light meal three to four hours before bedtime. Bananas and turkey both contain large amounts of tryptophan, a chemical that acts as a natural sedative.

Keep your bedroom cool: 16–21°C (61–68°F) is ideal. Warmer than that and you'll have a fitful night's sleep.

Caffeine and nicotine can prevent you from resting properly. Avoid them if possible, especially before bedtime. Alcohol may make you feel sleepy, but it will then disrupt the most restorative part of your night's sleep. Ensuing headaches and dehydration can also wake you up.

Save the bedroom for sleep and sex. Leave office work and homework for other rooms, otherwise you'll never be able to switch off from demanding projects.

Pure pampering Natural ways to get a good night's sleep

Having trouble nodding off at night? Before you reach for the sleeping pills, why not try one of these natural aids to rest and relaxation…

Valerian

A well-established alternative to conventional sleeping tablets, valerian is an effective herbal sedative. Once referred to as 'the Valium of the nineteenth century', it has been shown by research to be as effective as benzodiazepines (chemical tranquillizers) in treating insomnia, but has markedly fewer side effects. Available in tincture or powdered-root form, this herb is widely used in Europe as an aid to sleep and is often the main ingredient in over-the-counter natural sleep remedies.

IMPORTANT: Valerian should not be used if you're pregnant or breastfeeding, or when driving or operating machinery. If you are taking conventional drugs for hypertension (high blood pressure), sleeping pills or sedatives, consult your doctor before trying valerian.

Aromatherapy

Certain essential oils act on the nervous system, having a sedating or calming effect. Add a few drops of Roman chamomile, ylang ylang, sandalwood, neroli or clary sage to a warm bath, or place a few drops of lavender on a handkerchief and tuck it into your pillow before lights out. You can also make a bedtime body rub with 3 drops each of lavender, Roman chamomile and rose in 2 teaspoons of light carrier oil (not suitable for under-12s). For under-12s and babies, use just 1 drop of Roman chamomile or lavender in 2 teaspoons of sweet almond oil.

Sleepy teas

Chamomile makes one of the most famous sleep-inducing teas and many people swear by it. Drink a cup of chamomile tea at dinner-time and then another one hour before bedtime – any more than that and your bladder will keep you awake. Limeflower, catnip, lemon balm, passionflower and pre-prepared sleep teas (such as E-Teas 'Sleep and Nerves' blend or Dr Stuart's Tranquillity tea) will also help you doze off naturally.

Vitamins and minerals

Certain vitamins and minerals calm the nerves. Calcium, for example, is thought to induce sleep, and should be taken in the form of calcium citrate or calcium hydroxyapatite, according to holistic health expert Susan Clark. A nutritional therapist might also recommend increasing your intake of magnesium and vitamins B6 and B12.

Scented baths

A warm bath before bedtime will relax any tense muscles and help you unwind from a stressful day. Add scented herbs to the water and you'll enhance the soothing properties of a long soak.

Karena Callen, health and beauty director of *Red* magazine, suggests you should make a 'Desert Journey Bath Tea', created by the Westward Look Resort in Arizona, USA. Mix 1 tablespoon each of dried rose petals, citrus peel, lavender, rosemary, chamomile and sage with 10 drops of lavender essential oil. Store this mixture in a sealed glass jar, kept away from sunlight, and when you feel the need to relax simply add 2 heaped tablespoons to a square of muslin cloth, tie into a pouch and place under running bath water to steep for a few minutes before climbing in.

Bach Flower Remedies

Bach Flower Remedies are homeopathically prepared plant- and flower-based remedies, each one specifically designed to treat a different feeling. Their efficacy is yet to be proven by the scientific world, but many people report finding them helpful.

To aid sleep, try White Chestnut (if worrying is keeping you awake), Star of Bethlehem (if your insomnia follows an emotional shock) or Rock Rose (for stress-related sleeplessness). Rescue Remedy, a mix of five different remedies (Cherry Plum, Clematis, Impatiens, Rock Rose and Star of Bethlehem), may also combat insomnia due to nervous restlessness.

Eating for sleep

A glass of milk before bedtime: an old wives' tale or a guaranteed snooze inducer?

Research suggests that certain foods can actually contribute to restful sleep. These special 'sleeper' foods contain an amino acid called tryptophan, which the body uses to make the relaxing chemicals that help you get to sleep.

Dairy products not only contain plenty of tryptophan but are also packed with calcium, another sleep-inducing substance. This explains why a glass of milk is one of the best 'sleeper' foods around. Other foods high in tryptophan include pecan nuts, bananas, turkey, sesame and sunflower seeds.

But it's not only what you eat, but when you eat that helps or hinders sleep. Light evening meals promote a better night's rest than large blow-outs before bedtime. That's because all the digestive work required to process a big meal affects the quality of your sleep and can cause intermittent waking, even if it initially makes you feel drowsy.

IMPORTANT: If you are suffering from chronic insomnia, visit your doctor or a professional alternative practitioner who will be able to offer a more long-term solution.

PURE LIVING PRIORITY
If you do only one thing…
…invest in the best naturally filled mattress you can afford.

9

DIY

People who care about organic food and natural beauty often don't realize that they bring synthetic chemicals into their homes via paints, flooring and fabrics. But it's easy to see why. While almost every supermarket stocks eco-friendlier food and body-care ranges, finding healthier DIY products can be like looking for the proverbial needle in a haystack. However, simply by incorporating more natural materials into your home, and reducing the amount of synthetic paints and finishes you use, you'll create a living space that's both beautiful and healthy.

Paints

Conventional paints have come under fire in recent years. According to a Spanish study published in the *Lancet* medical journal, professional painters are five times more likely to have asthma than people in other occupations. More worryingly, scientists working for the World Health Organization also discovered that painters have lung cancer rates 40 per cent above the national average.

This is because synthetic paints contain solvents that can give off harmful volatile organic compounds (see 'What are…VOCs?', below). These toxic vapours are released not only when you apply the paint, but also as the paint dries and sometimes for years afterwards. A study in the USA by Johns Hopkins University, for example, showed that conventional paint contained 300 toxic chemicals, 150 of which are known to be carcinogenic. Conventional paint is likely to contain fungicides and heavy metals such as cadmium too,

What are… VOCs?

Volatile organic compounds (VOCs) are chemical compounds that evaporate easily into the air, especially in humid conditions. Formaldehyde is probably the most common VOC you'll find in your house, but others include benzene (from tobacco smoke, stored fuels and paint) and methylene chloride (found in paint strippers, adhesive removers, and aerosol spray paints).

VOCs are present in many different household products – from paints and laminate flooring to carpets and glues. According to the US Environmental Protection Agency (EPA), studies have shown that levels of some VOCs average two to five times higher indoors than outdoors. During and for several hours immediately after certain activities, such as paint stripping, levels indoors may be 1000 times background outdoor levels.

The EPA states that the health effects of VOCs are wide-ranging, from eye, nose, and throat irritation to more serious problems. The ability of VOCs to cause health effects is greatly influenced by factors such as level and length of exposure, but as a precautionary measure, the EPA advises that you:

1. Use household products according to manufacturers' directions.
2. Make sure that fresh air can circulate when using these products.
3. Don't store unused or little-used containers; buy in quantities that you will use up in one go.
4. Keep household products out of the reach of children and pets.
5. Never mix household products unless directed on the label.

which present a potential health risk as well as damaging the environment. Some paints, for example, contain bis(tributyltin) oxide (TBTO), a tin extract used as a fungicide. This compound can trigger irritation of the eyes, throat, skin and respiratory system and, as a result the US Environmental Protection Agency now recommends that you don't use TBTO paints in the interior of a home, although they appear to be safe for outside use.

PURE LIVING SOLUTION: The occasional use of conventional paint doesn't represent the same serious health risks as prolonged exposure. However, if you care about the air quality in your home and want to avoid problems traditionally associated with paint fumes, such as headaches or nausea, choose less toxic alternatives. Most DIY stores now stock low-VOC paint, which is an improvement on older varieties, but wherever possible try to use natural paints.

Natural paints are usually made from renewable, eco-friendly ingredients such as linseed oil or shellac resin and coloured with non-toxic natural pigments. They're also non-polluting and take less energy and fewer raw materials to produce. Companies such as Nutshell, Ecos, Georgina Barrow and Potmolen Paint produce a wide variety of ecologically sound and healthy paints, ranging from bog-standard emulsion to specialist distempers. These can cost a little more than conventional paints, so if your budget is tight prioritize the rooms where you and your children spend most time – that is, bedrooms and the nursery. If you do use conventional paint, or even low-VOC paint, make sure you work with the windows fully open and allow the room to ventilate for several days before moving back in. If you have any paint left at the end, don't throw it away (which causes more pollution); Community Repaint (see www.communityrepaint.org.uk) will put it to good use, collecting leftover reusable paint from householders and redistributing it to community projects.

Wallpaper

If you've been reading interior-design magazines lately, you'll know that wallpaper is officially 'back'. This is good news for those of us with uneven walls, but certain types of wallpaper might not be suitable for everyone. Vinyl wallpaper has been criticized for containing PVC, a plastic that poses major health and environmental hazards in its manufacture, product life and disposal, according to the Healthy Building Network (www.healthybuilding.net). Like synthetic paint, vinyl wallpaper can continue to release chemical vapours well into its life, causing irritation to people sensitive to chemicals. Plastic-coated wallpaper can also stop your walls from breathing, causing structural problems in the long run, while the synthetic dyes and fungicides found in traditional wallpaper are also unpopular with eco-building specialists.

EXPERT ADVICE Elizabeth's eco paints and finishes

 Elizabeth Wilhide is the author of many acclaimed books on house design and interiors, including *Eco: An Essential Sourcebook for Environmentally Friendly Design and Decoration*. A passionate believer that interiors can be both beautiful and healthy, she has this advice for anyone considering picking up a paintbrush:

- 'Select the least harmful option: choose natural or casein paints over synthetic paints. Do without finishes wherever possible. Exposed brick does not need finishing, while plasterwork can be left exposed and sealed with natural wax to prevent dusting.'

- 'Avoid polyurethane seals and varnishes for interior wood surfaces and flooring. Use linseed oil, tung oil or beeswax instead.'

- 'Keep rooms well ventilated during the application of paints or varnishes, wear protective clothing and masks and test samples before use to identify possible adverse reactions.'

- 'Light-toned paint reflects light and so reduces dependence on artificial light sources.'

- 'Lead is highly toxic but was once a common additive in paint. It is now banned in many parts of the world, including the USA, Britain and Australia. Old paintwork may contain lead, so extreme care should be taken when stripping it away. You may need professional help.'

Extract from *Eco* by Elizabeth Wilhide. Text copyright © Elizabeth Wilhide 2002, published by Quadrille Publishing Ltd.

PURE LIVING SOLUTION: An easy solution to this problem is to use thick lining paper (preferably recycled) and paint the surface with natural paints. This way, you get all the benefits of wallpaper without any of the potential chemical problems. For rooms where washable vinyl wallpaper is especially appropriate (such as bathrooms and kitchens), try using ceramic tiles or wipeable eco-emulsion instead (see 'Useful addresses', pages 129–37). To hang wallpaper, look for a fungicide-free paste such as Holzweg wallpaper paste.

Wood, fibreboards and MDF

Solid wood can be expensive. It's also prone to warping in certain weather conditions. To solve this problem, manufacturers came up with fibreboard. This wood-like material is made from small wood particles, often sawdust or wood chips, which are glued or pressed together to form large boards. It comes in different forms, including chipboard and medium-density fibreboard (MDF). Not only is fibreboard cheaper than solid wood, because it uses the bits of wood that no one wants, but it is actually more stable than normal timber (which continues to move throughout its life in response to humidity). Nowadays, fibreboard is everywhere in the home – from floors and coffee tables to kitchen units and built-in wardrobes.

However, despite all its useful qualities, fibreboard has one main drawback: formaldehyde. Formaldehyde resin is used to glue together the constituent parts in fibreboard and continues to emit vapours after manufacture. As we have seen in earlier chapters, this toxic VOC is an irritant even at low levels to the eyes, mucous membranes, nose and throat. It can also trigger dermatitis, asthma and rhinitis. In fact, such is the potential health risk that some building companies now recommend that clients use formaldehyde-free fibreboard in environmentally sensitive areas such as hospitals, nursing homes, nurseries and schools.

PURE LIVING SOLUTION: The National Society for Clean Air and Environmental Protection recommends that you should use low-emitting-formaldehyde wood products for any building work. You can buy formaldehyde-free MDF from many DIY superstores and it is marketed under several trade names including Medex and Medite II (see www.willamette-europe.com for stockists) and AllGreen. Eco-friendlier alternatives are springing up all the time – you can even buy a high-grade emission-free fibreboard made from wheat straw called PrimeBoard (www.primeboard.com).

If you do use normal fibreboard, make sure you paint or seal such products with a natural varnish to prevent any further emissions. Where possible, use a safer, more natural product such as solid wood or plywood (which has much lower concentrations of formaldehyde than fibreboard or MDF).

If you are using natural wood in the home, remember to check that it comes from a sustainable source. Look for the Forest Stewardship Council (FSC) logo – this will tell you that your wood comes from a well-managed forest. If you want to be eco-friendly, it's also important to use local and recycled timber where possible and avoid timber from endangered species including teak, rosewood, ebony, ramin and mahogany. For more information, consult Friends of the Earth's *The Good Wood Guide*.

Sawdust, whether it's from fibreboard or natural wood, can also trigger health problems. Hardwood dust, for example, has been implicated in causing nasal cancer and all wood dusts can irritate the respiratory system. If you are doing any kind of DIY activity that produces sawdust, it's absolutely vital to wear a mask and work in a well-ventilated area.

Wood finishes

Conventional varnishes suffer from the same problem as paints – namely, high levels of VOCs. For a healthier and more ecologically sound alternative, use a natural wood finish such as linseed oil or beeswax. You can also buy specially prepared natural wood finishes and waxes, for every type of external and internal surface, from suppliers like Construction Resources and the Green Building Store.

Paint stripping

If you plan to do any paint stripping and your house was built before the 1950s, you may find yourself dealing with layers of old lead paint. Lead is very dangerous whether ingested or inhaled, so you have to take great care, especially around children, if you want to remove it. More information on lead in old paint is available from the Department for the Environment website (see page 129).

For removing all other types of paint and varnish, you can use Homestrip from Eco Solutions, an award-winning water-based stripper that you just paint on and leave to do its magic. Unlike conventional paint stripper, it's non-toxic, non-flammable, and solvent-free.

What is...asbestos?

Asbestos was commonly used in the past as a building material because it was very efficient as fire-proofing and insulation. Unfortunately, it also turned out to be lethal. Asbestos fibres are dangerous if inhaled, causing scarring of the lung tissue (fibrosis), and lung, chest and abdominal cancers. Asbestos stopped being used as a building material in the 1980s, but if you find it in your home, it's important that you leave it alone and contact the Environmental Health Department of your local council, which will establish whether it needs to be removed professionally. The Health and Safety Executive (www.hse.gov.uk/asbestos) has a website dedicated to the problem of asbestos and how to remove it safely: http://www.nsca.org.uk/leaf3.htm.

Pure shopping
The Green Building Store

Despite the hidden health risks in many of today's building materials, it can be difficult to find alternatives at your local DIY superstore. Thanks to companies like the Green Building Store, however, less toxic products are now within the reach of every home improver.

FOR MORE INFORMATION, see 'Useful addresses', page 134.

Passionate and knowledgeable about eco-friendly, healthy buildings, the company's founders, Bill Butcher, Chris Herring and Steve Slator, created an online and mail-order business supplying everything a 'green builder' could want – from natural gloss paints and brush cleaners to environmentally sensitive windows, doors and conservatories – all under one roof.

As with many eco-friendly enterprises, the company practises what it preaches. The Green Building Store's award-winning company offices include energy-efficient windows and doors, natural paints and wood finishes, as well as being supplied with electricity by renewable energy. All three directors are also long-standing members of the Association for Environment-Conscious Building, while Bill and Steve designed and built the Longwood low-energy house in Huddersfield, one of the most energy efficient in the UK.

Newly built houses
may be the worst
culprits for indoor
air pollution.
The Commonwealth
Scientific and
Industrial Research
Organization (CSIRO)
in Australia found that
houses less than one
year old had up to
20 times the safe limit
of volatile organic
compounds (VOCs)
recommended by
the National Health
and Medical Research
Council. When a
similar study was
undertaken in
England, one fifth
of new homes were
found to have levels
at least twice the safe
limit. The hazardous
chemicals seemed
to be leaking from
furniture, floors and
freshly painted walls
and, although not a
grave threat to human
health, could lead to
headaches, breathing
difficulties or other
VOC-related problems.

Flooring

Ninety per cent of Britons have carpets in their homes, but hard floors may be better for your health. Wall-to-wall carpets harbour toxins at levels up to ten times higher than those found on polluted urban streets, according to research published by *New Scientist* magazine. US environmental engineer John Roberts found that the average ten-year-old carpet will store 900g (2lb) of dust containing high concentrations of heavy metals, pesticides and polycyclic aromatic hydrocarbons (PAHs), a group of highly carcinogenic chemicals that are released when certain substances are burnt. Children are more at risk from these toxins than adults because they often play and crawl on the floor. John Roberts makes the point: 'If truckloads of dust with the same concentration of toxic chemicals as is found in most carpets were deposited outside, these locations would be considered hazardous waste dumps.'

But how do the toxins get into the carpet? Dirt is walked into your carpet from outside, leaving traces of soil, pollen, car-exhaust dust, soot, animal waste products, pesticides, mould spores and other contaminants. Combine that with the chemicals that are already added to carpet in the manufacturing process, including fire retardants, styrene (a suspected carcinogen) and chlorinated paraffins, and it's no wonder carpet has been dubbed a 'toxic sponge'.

Carpets also harbour dust mites, a disaster for any asthma sufferer. Once in place, dust mites in carpets are hard to shift as chemical sprays and air-filtering systems have little effect. A report published at the University of Southampton confirmed that carpets harbour asthma-promoting allergens from dust mites, while researchers at the Manchester Asthma and Allergy Study Group found that 'environmental manipulation', which included removing carpets in bedrooms, reduced asthma and other allergy symptoms in high-risk babies.

PURE LIVING SOLUTION: If you love your carpet and can't bear to part with it, make sure you vacuum regularly (at least once a day) to remove as much of the potentially dangerous dust as possible. Ensure that people wipe their feet on the doormat and get them to take their shoes off when they're inside the house.

If it's time to replace your carpet, consider hard flooring instead. Natural wood floors, linoleum, ceramic tiles, cork and formaldehyde-free laminate floors look great and can be combined with washable rugs if you want to soften the look. A house with hard floors will also have only 10 per cent of the dust found in a house with wall-to-wall carpet, which is much better for asthma sufferers. Avoid PVC (vinyl) flooring if you can, however, as it can contain phthalates (see page 22) and chlorinated paraffins, and may emit harmful vapours during its life.

If you want the warmth and sound insulation of carpet, you can buy natural versions that don't contain synthetic chemicals or formaldehyde-impregnated backing. Coir, jute and organic wool carpets are all healthy, eco-friendlier options and you can even buy a woven or woollen felt backing rather than a synthetic one. For more information, the Healthy Flooring Network (www.healthyflooring.org) has a very helpful online guide.

What is...radon?

Radon is a natural radioactive gas that rises from rocks and soil. You can't taste, see or smell it but it can be detected with special devices. Radon doesn't present a problem outside the home, but when it becomes trapped inside a house it poses a serious risk to health, damaging your lung tissue and putting you at an increased risk of developing lung cancer. Concentrations of radon vary from place to place, with many areas experiencing only low levels. However, limestone areas such as Derbyshire, north Oxfordshire, Northamptonshire, Somerset and Lincolnshire, and granite areas such as Cornwall and Devon, are at risk from higher levels of radon.

The government recommends that people living in these high-risk areas test their houses for radon. Your local council should have more information on the radon levels in your area. Estate agents and solicitors are also becoming more aware of radon issues, so if you are thinking of moving house or extending your property in a high-risk area, there are steps you can take to reduce the risk of a radon problem. If tests do confirm that your house has high levels of radon, don't panic. See the National Radiological Protection Board (www.nrpb.org) for more information and resources on testing for, and tackling, radon.

PVC and PVC-u

You'll find PVC in virtually every home – in windows, flooring, pipes, tables, chairs, conservatories – but increasing demand is being placed on governments to phase it out of use. As a material it scores pretty badly on the environmental and health front: the production and disposal of PVC-u window frames, for example, involves six of the fifteen toxic chemicals European governments are attempting to phase out (dioxins, furans, lead, cadmium, mercury and organic tin compounds). PVC can also continue to emit harmful VOC vapours well into its life.

Fortunately there are other, safer materials you can use. Why not build a hardwood conservatory, for instance, rather than one made from PVC-u, or use clay underground pipes instead of plastic? Sounds impractical? The Sydney 2000 Olympics managed to avoid PVC in the seating, floor coverings and plumbing of the entire stadium. Where natural materials are not appropriate, other, less polluting plastics can take the place of PVC. According to Greenpeace, polyethylene- or polypropylene-based plastics are recyclable and less polluting, with companies such as Internorm (www.internorm.com) and Trocal (www.trocal-profiles.com) both producing PVC-free plastic window frames.

Upholstery and fabrics

For upholstery, curtains and other fabrics around the home look for organic or unbleached cotton, wool, hemp and linen. Conventional cotton and wool production involves the heavy use of chemicals, some of which will still be on the fabric by the time it reaches your home. If organic fabrics are too expensive or difficult to find, make sure you buy washable materials and give them a few rinses in the washing machine before you use them. The same goes for bedding, towels and throws. Look for fabrics that are naturally dyed or retain their original colour – muted natural shades have an innate elegance and are very comforting to live with (see 'Useful addresses', pages 129–37, for suppliers).

Green building

If you want to find out more about eco-friendly DIY, there are a number of organizations that can help. The Centre for Alternative Technology offers free information, a mail-order service for books and products, and residential courses for anyone interested in green building. You might find Eco Construction (www.ecoconstruction.org) and the Association of Environment-Conscious Building (www.aecb.net) useful too. There are also two books that are the bibles for any green builder or decorator: David Pearson's wonderful *The Natural House Book*, and *The Whole House Book* by Pat Borer and Cindy Harris.

The finishing touches

Unless you are planning to build a new house from scratch, creating a more natural, organic home will be a gradual process. It isn't realistic to change the whole interior of a home in one go, but think about investing in low-tox furniture and finishings next time you redecorate. For instance, when the bedroom is due to be repainted or your old sofa has finally given up the ghost, that's the time to look around for eco-friendlier, low-chemical alternatives.

Pure Living isn't supposed to be prescriptive about what your house should look like, but there are definitely ingredients that go together to create a more natural, healthy home. We've looked at many of these in this and other chapters, but to summarize you might want to be thinking about the following elements:

- Keep things simple and in the most natural state possible.
- Enjoy the beauty of stripped wooden floors and natural paints on the walls.

- Use naturally derived materials as often as possible – wood, stone, glass, cork, bamboo, ceramic tiles – all these materials have an integrity and elegance that will make your home feel comfy and cosy and help you feel more in tune with your living space.
- Avoid using too many synthetic materials such as PVC-u, vinyl or MDF.
- Encourage natural light to stream into your home and create focal points with real wood-burning stoves.
- Create quiet spaces and banish unwanted noise from your home.
- Encourage calming scents and sounds into your living space.
- Use antiques, salvage and second-hand materials and furniture where possible – they not only have bags of character but they're probably also made from better-quality, less chemically treated materials than modern equivalents.
- Don't have too much technology – an overdose of home-entertainment systems, stereos, computers, printers, faxes and photocopiers can make your home feel uncomfortable and potentially cause health problems.
- In the day-to-day running of the home, avoid chemically laden household cleaners, bath products, cosmetics and food. Watch out for clutter and dust traps.
- Use fabrics and upholstery which come from natural, preferably organic sources – cotton, wool, hemp, silk, leather, linen and hessian. Layer fabrics to create luxury and look for naturally dyed or unbleached products.
- Accessorize with natural materials and *objets trouvés* – pebbles, driftwood, candles, feathers, plants and flowers.

PURE LIVING PRIORITY

If you do only one thing...
...use natural paints in the bedroom and the nursery.

Useful addresses

Organizations, charities and government bodies

About Organics
Website: www.aboutorganics.co.uk
Complete organic information resource

Agency for Toxic Substances and Disease Registry
E-mail: ATSDRIC@cdc.gov
Website: www.atsdr.cdc.gov
Health information to prevent harmful exposure and disease related to toxic substances

Association of Environment-Conscious Building
PO Box 32, LLandysul
SA44 5ZA
Website: www.aecb.net

British Snoring and Sleep Apnoea Association
2nd Floor Suite, 52 Albert Road North
Reigate, Surrey
RH2 9EL
Tel: 01737 245638
E-mail: info@britishsnoring.co.uk
Website: www.britishsnoring.com

Children's Health Environmental Coalition
PO Box 1540, Princeton
NJ 08542
USA
E-mail: chec@checnet.org
Website: www.checnet.org
US children's charity campaigning against toxic substances in homes, schools and communities

Community Repaint
Website: www.communityrepaint.org.uk

Consumers' Association
2 Marylebone Road
London
NW1 4DF
Website: www.which.net/campaigns/contents.html
Campaigns on key consumer issues

Department for the Environment, Food and Rural Affairs
Website: www.defra.gov.uk

Forest Stewardship Council
Unit D, Station Buildings
Llanidloes, Powys
SY18 6EB
Tel: 01686 413916
E-mail: info@fsc-uk.org
Website: www.fsc-uk.info

Friends of the Earth
26–28 Underwood Street
London
N1 7JQ
Tel: 020 7490 1555
Website: www.foe.org.uk

Greenpeace
Canonbury Villas
London
N1 2PN
Tel: 020 7865 8100
E-mail: info@uk.greenpeace.org
Website: www.greenpeace.org.uk

Health and Safety Executive
HSE Infoline
Caerphilly Business Park
Caerphilly
CF83 3GG
Tel: Infoline 08701 545500
E-mail: hseinformationservices@natbrit.com
Website: www.hse.gov.uk
'One-stop shop' government website for health and safety information

Healthy Building Network

Institute for Local Self-Reliance
927 15th Street, NW, 4th Floor
Washington DC 20005
USA
E-mail: info@healthybuilding.net
Website: www.healthybuilding.net
US network of green building professionals, environmental and health activists

Healthy Flooring Network

PO Box 30626
London
E1 1TZ
Tel: 020 7481 9004
E-mail: info@healthyflooring.org
Website: www.healthyflooring.org

The Hyperactive Children's Support Group

Dept W., 71 Whyke Lane
Chichester
West Sussex
PO19 7PD
Tel: 01243 551313
E-mail: hyperactive@hacsg.org.uk
Website: www.hacsg.org.uk

London Hazards Centre

Hampstead Town Hall Centre
213 Haverstock Hill
London
NW3 4QP
Tel: 020 7794 5999
E-mail: mail@lhc.org.uk
Website: www.lhc.org.uk
UK health and safety resource

National Association of Farmers' Markets

PO Box 575
Southampton
SO15 7BZ
Tel: 0845 230 2150
Website: www.farmersmarkets.net
Promoting and supporting farmers' markets – website includes a full list of farmers' markets across the UK

National Radiological Protection Board

Chilton, Didcot
Oxfordshire
OX11 0RQ
Tel: 01235 831600
E-mail: nrpb@nrpb.org
Website: www.nrpb.org

National Safe Kids Campaign

1301 Pennsylvania Ave, NW
Suite 1000
Washington DC 20004
USA
Website: www.safekids.org
Promoting child safety to prevent accidental injury

National Sleep Foundation

1522 K Street, NW
Suite 500
Washington DC 20005
USA
Website: www.sleepfoundation.org
Information on sleep disorders and sleep-related research

National Society for Clean Air and Environmental Protection

44 Grand Parade
Brighton
BN2 9QA
Tel: 01273 878770
E-mail: admin@nsca.org.uk
Website: www.nsca.org.uk
Promotes clean air and environmental protection through the reduction of air, water and land pollution, noise and other contaminants

Organic Food

Website: www.organicfood.co.uk
Online magazine about organic food and shopping – includes a list of organic shops, box schemes and mail order nationwide

Pesticide Action Network UK
Eurolink Centre
Unit 16, 49 Effra Road
London
SW2 1BZ
Tel: 020 7274 8895
E-mail: admin@pan-uk.org
Website: www.pan-uk.org
Promotes healthy food and pesticide-free agriculture

Real Nappy Association
PO Box 3704
London
SE26 4RX
Tel: 020 8299 4519
UK Nappy Helpline: 01983 401959
Website: www.nappyline.org.uk
E-mail: nappy@wrap.org.uk
Complete resource on eco-friendly nappies

SAD Association
PO Box 989
Steyning
BN44 3HG
Website: www.sada.org.uk
*Support organization for people suffering with seasonal
affective disorder*

Soil Association
Bristol House, 40–56 Victoria Street
Bristol
BS1 6BY
Tel: 0117 314 5000
E-mail: info@soilassociation.org
Website: www.soilassociation.org.uk
*Organic food, farming and certification. Website includes
an organic directory with all the box delivery schemes
around Britain*

UK Building Research Establishment
Garston, Watford
WD25 9XX
Tel: 01923 664000
E-mail: enquiries@bre.co.uk
Website: www.bre.co.uk
*Leading centre of expertise on buildings, construction,
energy, environment, fire and risk*

US Environmental Protection Agency
Ariel Rios Building
1200 Pennsylvania Avenue, NW
Washington DC 20460
USA
Website: www.epa.gov
*Information on the latest developments in environmental
science and human health research*

Women's Environmental Network (WEN)
PO Box 30626
London
E1 1TZ
Tel: 020 7481 9004
E-mail: info@wen.org.uk
Website: www.wen.org.uk
Campaigning on environmental and health issues

WWF – UK
Panda House, Weyside Park
Godalming, Surrey
GU7 1XR
Tel: 01483 426444
Website: www.wwf.org.uk

Online retailers, mail-order companies and shops

Abel & Cole
8–15 MGI Estate
Milkwood Road
London
SE24 0JF
Tel: 020 7737 3648 or 0845 262 6262
E-mail: organics@abel-cole.co.uk
Website: www.abel-cole.co.uk
Organic food home-delivery service

Alphabeds
92 Tottenham Court Road
London
W1T 4TL
Tel: 020 7636 6840
E-mail: enquiries@alphabeds.co.uk
Website: www.alphabeds.co.uk
Wooden bedframes and organic mattresses

Angela Wright
Colour Affects
908 Keyes House, Dolphin Square
London
SW1V 3NB
Tel: 020 8932 6492
E-mail: info@colour-affects.co.uk
Website: www.colour-affects.co.uk
Colour psychology website and practice

Aromantic
17 Tytler Street
Forres, Moray
IV36 1EL
Scotland
Tel: 01309 696900
E-mail: info@aromantic.co.uk
Website: www.aromantic.co.uk
Sells ingredients to make your own natural beauty products

As Nature Intended
201 Chiswick High Road
London
W4 2DR
Tel: 020 8742 8838
E-mail: enquiries@asnatureintended.uk.com
Website: www.asnatureintended.uk.com
Organic foods, vitamins and lifestyle products

Auro Organic Paints
Holbrook Garage
Cheltenham Road
Bisley, Stroud
Gloucestershire
GL6 7BX
Tel: 01452 772020
E-mail: sales@auroorganic.co.uk
Website: www.auroorganic.co.uk
Natural DIY paints

Aveda
28–29 Marylebone High Street
London
W1U 4PL
Tel: 020 7224 3157
Website: www.aveda.com
Natural hair-care, skin-care and make-up

Bach Flower Remedies
A. Nelson & Co. Ltd
Broadheath House
83 Parkside, Wimbledon
London
SW19 5LP
Website: www.bachessences.com

Bio-D
Unit 2
Chapman Street Industrial Estate
Kingston upon Hull
HU8 7BU
Tel: 01482 229950
E-mail: bio-d@ecodet.karoo.co.uk
Website: www.biodegradable.biz
Natural cleaning products

Boots the Chemist
Tel: 0845 070 8090
Website: www.boots.com
Organic babyfoods, milk, reusable nappies and anti-allergy products

Cariad
PO Box 2108
Bristol
BS99 7RL
Tel: 0870 350 1095
E-mail: email@mycariad.com
Website: www.mycariad.com
Aromatherapy products

The Ceramic Stove Company
4 Earl Street
Oxford
OX2 0JA
Tel: 01865 245077
E-mail: info@ceramicstove.com
Website: www.ceramicstove.com
Wood-burning stoves

Clothworks
PO Box 3233
Bradford upon Avon
BA15 2WB
Tel: 01225 309218
E-mail: info@clothworks.co.uk
Website: www.clothworks.co.uk
Eco-textiles, clothing, bedding and nappies

Construction Resources
16 Great Guildford Street
London
SE1 OHS
Tel: 020 7450 2211
E-mail: sales@ecoconstruct.com
Website: www.constructionresources.com
Ecological building resource centre and shop

Cotton Bottoms
7–9 Water Lane Industrial Estate
Water Lane, Storrington
West Sussex
RH20 3XX
Tel: 0870 777 8899
E-mail: sales@cottonbottoms.co.uk
Website: www.cottonbottoms.co.uk
Eco-friendly cotton nappies and laundry service

David Colwell Design
Trannon Studio
Llawryglyn, Caersws
Powys
SY17 5RH
Tel: 01686 430313
E-mail: info@davidcolwel.com
Website: www.davidcolwell.com
Eco-friendly, award-winning furniture for home and office

Dr Hauschka
Elysia Natural Skin Care
27 Stockwood Business Park
Stockwood, Redditch
Worcestershire
B96 6SX
Tel: 01386 792622
E-mail: enquiries@drhauschka.co.uk
Website: www.drhauschka.co.uk
Biodynamic and organic skin-care, hair-care and make-up

Eastbrook Farms Organic Meat
The Calf House, Cues Lane
Bishopstone, Swindon
Wiltshire
SN6 8PL
Tel: 01793 790340
E-mail: info@helenbrowningorganics.co.uk
Website: www.helenbrowningorganics.co.uk
Mail-order organic meat, delivered nationwide

Eco Solutions
Summerleaze House
Church Road, Winscombe
North Somerset
BS25 1BH
Tel: 01934 844484
E-mail: info@ecosolutions.co.uk
Website: www.ecosolutions.co.uk
Eco-friendly DIY products including paint stripper

Ecos Paints
Unit 34, Heysham Business Park
Middleton Road
Heysham
LA3 3PP
Tel: 01524 852371
Website: www.ecopaints.com
Odourless, solvent-free organic paints

Ecover
E-mail: info.ecover@greenhq.co.ukm
Website: www.ecover.com
Eco-friendly cleaning products

E-Teas
Tel: 01539 558924
E-mail: info@e-teas.co.uk
Website: www.e-teas.co.uk
Natural teas and infusions

Fresh & Wild
49 Parkway
London
NW1 7PN
Tel: 020 7428 7575
Website: www.freshandwild.com
Organic foods and natural remedies

Georgina Barrow
Camp Farm
Farmington
Cheltenham
GL54 3NG
Tel: 01451 861040
Website: www.naturalpaints.org.uk
Traditional and eco-paints

Goodness Direct
South March
Daventry
Northants
NN11 4PH
Tel: 0871 871 6611
E-mail: info@goodnessdirect.co.uk
Website: www.goodnessdirect.co.uk
Mail-order organic food with nationwide delivery

Green & Black's
E-mail: enquiries@greenandblacks.com
Website: www.greenandblacks.com
Organic chocolatiers

Green Baby
345 Upper Street
Islington
London
N1 0PD
Tel: 0870 240 6894
E-mail: info@greenbaby.co.uk
Website: www.greenbaby.co.uk
Wide range of mail-order natural baby products and eco-friendly nappies

Green Building Store
11 Huddersfield Road
Meltham, Holmfirth
West Yorkshire
HD9 4NJ
Tel: 01484 854898
E-mail: info@greenbuildingstore.co.uk
Website: www.greenbuildingstore.co.uk
Green building and DIY products

Green People
Brighton Road
Handcross
West Sussex
RH17 6BZ
Tel: 08702 401444
E-mail: organic@greenpeople.co.uk
Website: www.greenpeople.co.uk
Organic body, skin, dental, baby and hair-care products plus home cleaning products

The Green Shop
Cheltenham Road
Bisley, Stroud
Gloucestershire
GL6 7BX
Tel: 01452 770629
E-mail: enquiries@greenshop.co.uk
Website: www.greenshop.co.uk
Includes household products, body-care products and stationery

The Green Stationery Company
Studio One, 114 Walcot Street
Bath
BA1 5BG
Tel: 01225 480556
E-mail: jay@greenstat.co.uk
Website: www.greenstat.co.uk
Eco-friendly office supplies

Greenfibres
99 High Street
Totnes
Devon
TQ9 5PF
Tel: 01803 868001
E-mail: mail@greenfibres.com
Website: www.greenfibres.com
Organic baby clothing, bedding, nightwear, skin-care and home products

Hawkshead Organic Trout Farm
The Boathouse
Ridding Wood, Hawkshead
Cumbria
LA22 0QF
Tel: 01539 436541
E-mail: trout@hawkshead.demon.co.uk
Website: www.organicfish.com
Mail-order organically reared fish

Healing Products

Margaret Evans
Camomile House
Horseshoe Close
Ruskington
NG34 9DB
Tel: 01526 832491
E-mail: well77@aol.com
Website: www.healingproduct.co.uk
*Complementary healing products including SK
eczema cream*

The Healthy House

The Old Co-op
Lower Street, Ruscombe
Stroud
GL6 6BU
Tel: 01453 752216
E-mail: info@healthy-house.co.uk
Website: www.healthy-house.co.uk
Products for a healthy home

Hipp

165 Main Street
New Greenham Park, Newbury
Berkshire
RG19 6HN
Tel: 0845 050 1351
E-mail: inforequest@hipp.co.uk
Website: www.hipp.co.uk
Organic babyfoods and formulas

Honeybee Gardens

1082 Palisades Drive
Leesport
PA 19533
USA
E-mail: sales@honeybeegardens.com
Website: www.honeybeegardens.com
All natural, herbal body-care products and cosmetics

Jurlique

Naturopathic Health and Wellness Centres
Holly House, 300–302 Chiswick High Road
London
W4 1NP
Tel: 08707 700980
E-mail: info@jurlique.com
Website: www.jurlique.com
Natural skin-care range

Kingfisher Toothpaste

White Lodge Estate
Hall Road
Norwich
NR4 6DG
Tel: 01603 630484
E-mail: richard@kingfishertoothpaste.com
Website: www.kingfishertoothpaste.com
Natural toothpaste

The Little Big Food Company

74 Lairgate
Beverley
East Yorkshire
HU17 8EU
Tel: 01482 889 630
E-mail: tony@thelittlebigfoodcompany.co.uk
Website: www.thelittlebigfoodcompany.co.uk
*Organic frozen food and prepared meals
(with a great website!)*

Little Green Earthlets

Unit 17, Silveroaks Farm
Waldron
East Sussex
TN21 0RS
Tel: 08701 624462
E-mail: sales@earthlets.co.uk
Website: www.earthlets.co.uk
*Environmentally sound cotton nappies, baby skin-care,
pushchairs, baby clothing, toys, and feeding products*

Marks & Spencer

Tel: Customer Services 0845 302 1234
Website: www.marksandspencer.com
*Over 190 organic food products ranging from fresh fruit
and vegetables to snacks and sauces*

Natracare

Tel: 01275 371764
E-mail: info@natracare.com
Website: www.natracare.com
Organic GM-free cotton tampons

Natural Baby Company

PO Box 76
Ryde
Isle of Wight
PO33 3XH
Tel: 01983 810925
E-mail: info@naturalbaby.com
Website: www.naturalbabycompany.com
Eco-friendly disposable nappies

Natural Collection

PO Box 135
Southampton
Hampshire
SO14 0FQ
Tel: Customer Services 0870 331 3335
E-mail: info@naturalcollection.com
Website: www.naturalcollection.com
Everything you need for a natural, eco-friendly home

Neal's Yard Remedies

8–10 Ingate Place
Battersea
London
SW8 3NS
Tel: 020 7498 1686
E-mail: mail@nealsyardremedies.com
Website: www.nealsyardremedies.com
Aromatherapy, homoeopathy and herbalism. Body, skin, baby and hair-care

Nutshell Natural Paints

PO Box 72
South Brent
TQ10 9YR
Tel: 01364 73801
E-mail: info@nutshellpaints.com
Website: www.nutshellpaints.com
Eco-friendly paints

The Organic Delivery Company

68 Rivington Street
London
EC2A 3AY
Tel: 020 7739 8181
E-mail: info@organicdelivery.co.uk
Website: www.organicdelivery.co.uk
Delivery service for the London area

Organix

Freepost BH1 336
Christchurch
Dorset
BH23 2ZZ
Tel: 0800 393511
E-mail: lizzie.vann@organixbrands.com
Website: www.babyorganix.co.uk
Organic babyfoods and formulas

Original Fresh Babyfood Company

19–21 Dryden Vale
Bilston Glen
Midlothian
EH20 9HN
Tel: 0131 448 0440
E-mail: information@simplyorganic.co.uk
Website: www.simplyorganic.co.uk
Organic babyfoods and formulas

Out of This World

106 High Street
Gosforth
Newcastle
NE3 1HB
Tel: 0191 213 5377
E-mail: info@ootw.co.uk
Website: www.ootw.co.uk
Ethical and organic co-operative. Stores in Cheltenham, Newcastle and Nottingham

Paula Pryke Flowers

The Flower House
Cynthia Street
London
N1 9JF
Tel: 020 7837 7336
Website: www.paula-pryke-flowers.com
Cutting-edge flower arrangements and floristry courses

Planet Organic

42 Westbourne Grove
London
W2 5SH
Tel: 020 7221 7171
E-mail: sales@planetorganic.com
Website: www.planetorganic.com
Organic food and body-care products

Simply Nature Limited
7 Old Factory Buildings
Battenhurst Road
Stonegate, East Sussex
TN5 7DU
Tel: 01580 201687
E-mail: info@simply-nature.co.uk
Website: www.simply-nature.co.uk
Range of natural skin-care and cosmetics

Spirit of Nature
Unit 7, Hannah Way
Gordleton Industrial Park
Lymington
SO41 8JD
Tel: 0870 725 9885
E-mail: mail@spiritofnature.co.uk
Website: www.spiritofnature.co.uk
Extensive range of natural and environmentally friendly products

Textiles From Nature
84 Stoke Newington Church Street
London
N16 0AP
Tel: 020 7241 0990
Fax: 020 7241 1991
Website: www.textilesfromnature.com
Organic textiles, clothing towels and bedding

Vinceremos
74 Kirkgate
Leeds
LS2 7DJ
Tel: 0113 244 0002
E-mail: webinfo@vinceremos.co.uk
Website: www.vinceremos.co.uk
Over 300 organic wines beers, ciders, juices, cordials and spirits to buy online

Weleda
Heanor Road
Ilkeston
Derbyshire
DE7 8DR
Tel: 0115 944 8200
Website: www.weleda.co.uk
Anthroposophic and homoeopathic medicines and natural body-care products

Other useful websites

Guardian Unlimited
Website: www.guardian.co.uk
Archive of past articles

The Hyperactive Children's Support Group
Website: www.hacsg.org.uk

The Lancet
Website: www.thelancet.com
Medical research information and news

Linda Chaé
Website: www.lindachae.com
Information and research into safe, organic cosmetics and skin care products

New Scientist
Website: www.newscientist.com
Latest research news

Bibliography

Alexander, Jane (1998) *Detox Plan*

Berman, Alan (2001) *The Healthy Home Handbook*

Berry, Susan (1995) *The Colour Book*

Berthold-Bond, Annie (1999) *Better Basics for the Home*

Bird, Julia (2000) *The Naturally Scented Home*

Blake, Jill (1998) *Healthy Home*

Borer, Pat and Harris, Cindy (1998) *The Whole House Book*

Breecher M.P.H., Maury M., and Linde Ph.D, Shirley (1992) *Healthy Homes in a Toxic World*

Brewer, Dr Sarah (1991) *The Ultimate Stress Buster*

Brown, Lynda (2000) *Organic Living*

Brown, Lynda (2002) *The New Shopper's Guide to Organic Food*

Callard, Sarah and Millis, Diane (2001) *Green Living*

Callen, Karena (2001) *Spa*

Clark, Susan (2000) *What Really Works*

Conran, Terence (1994) *The Essential House Book*

Ethical Consumer Research Association, The (2002) *The Good Shopping Guide*

Friends of the Earth (1996) *Green Home Handbook*

Goldberg, Burton (1998) *Chronic Fatigue and Environmental Illness*

Good Housekeeping (2001) *Organic Handbook*

Hanan, Ali (2000) *Modern Rustic*

Hanan, Ali and Norris, Pip (2001) *Untouched: Using Natural Materials and Methods to Decorate Your Home*

Hanssen, Maurice (1987) *E for Additives*

Holford, Patrick (1997) *The Optimum Nutrition Bible*

Howarth, Dr Peter and Reid, Anita (2000) *Allergy-Free Living*

Landrigan M.D., Philip J., Needleman M.D., Herbert L. and Landrigan M.P.A., Mary (2001) *Raising Healthy Children in a Toxic World*

Lazenby, Gina (2000) *The Healthy Home*

Maceoin, Beth (1999) *Natural Medicine: A Practical Guide to Family Health*

Maxted-Frost, Tanyia (1999) *The Organic Baby Book*

McIntyre, Anne (1999) *Healing Drinks*

Neal's Yard Remedies (2000) *Natural Health and Body Care*

Palma Ph.D, Robert J. (1995) *The Complete Guide to Household Chemicals*

Pearson, David (1998) *The Natural House Book*

Petro Roybal, Beth Ann (2002) *101 Simple Ways to Make Your Home and Family Safe in A Toxic World*

Phillips, Dan (2000) *Good Housekeeping's The Eco Friendly Home*

Schmitz-Gunther, Thomas (1999) *Living Spaces: Sustainable Building and Design*

Scrivner, Jane (1998) *Detox Yourself*

Scrinver, Jane (1999) *Detox Your Life*

Selby, Anna (2001) *Home Health Sanctuary*

Seo, Danny (2001) *Conscious Style Home: Eco Friendly Living for the 21st Century*

Tanqueray, Rebecca (2000) *Eco Chic*

Van Straten, Michael (1999) *Organic Super Foods*

Walter, Dawna and Franks, Mark (2002) *The Life Laundry: How to De-Junk Your Life*

Wilhide, Elizabeth (2002) *Eco: An Essential Sourcebook*

Acknowledgements

I would very much like to thank all the people who helped *Pure Living* happen.

Viv Bowler, my Commissioning Editor, has my unreserved thanks for all her advice, encouragement and friendship right from the very start. Huge thanks also go to everyone at BBC Books – especially Samantha Wray, Sarah Lavelle, Sarah Ponder and Victoria Hall – for all their hard work and enthusiasm.

I am immensely grateful to all the experts who so kindly contributed to the book – Dr David Bull, Romy Fraser, Antony Worrall Thompson, Rose Elliot, Dawna Walter, Jill Barker, Paula Pryke, Linda Barker and Elizabeth Wilhide.

Thanks also go to Marks & Spencer, Dr Hauschka, Green & Black's, David Colwell Design, Cotton Bottoms, Natural Collection, Nutshell Paints, Greenfibres and the Green Building Store.

And finally, my special thanks go to my wonderful family and friends, especially Mum and Dad and my husband Alastair for their endless support, eagle-eyed proofreading and frothy coffee.

Picture credits

Index